RATIONAL DEFIANCE

Rational Defiance

A Guide to Clear Thinking, Bold Action, and
Living on Your Own Terms

Henk Pretorius, PhD

COPYRIGHT © 2026 HENK PRETORIUS, PHD
All rights reserved.

RATIONAL DEFIANCE
A Guide to Clear Thinking, Bold Action, and Living on Your Own Terms

FIRST EDITION

ISBN   978-1-5445-5011-4 *Hardcover*
          978-1-5445-5010-7 *Paperback*
          978-1-5445-5012-1 *Ebook*

To my parents, Lize, Elna, Ella and Avery

Contents

INTRODUCTION 9

PART I: THE CONFORMITY COMA
1. STUCK IN THE STATUS QUO 25
2. THE CONSISTENCY TRAP 41
3. THE COMPLIANCE TRAP 55
4. THE COMPLACENCY TRAP 71

PART II: THE DEFIANT MINDSET
5. RATIONAL DEFIANCE 85
6. SEE CLEARLY 101
7. SEEK RADICAL INPUTS 113
8. SAMPLE UNCONVENTIONAL EXPERIENCES 125

PART III: THE DEFIANT PATH
9. STAND FOR SOMETHING 139
10. SET YOUR COURSE 151
11. SILENCE DISTRACTIONS 163
12. STAY DEFIANT 175

CONCLUSION 187
NOTES 195

Introduction

Are You Swimming or Floating?

IN APRIL 1958, TWENTY-ONE-YEAR-OLD HUNTER S. THOMPSON wrote a letter to Hume Logan, a friend who had asked for life advice. This was years before Thompson became famous for his unconventional approach to writing and life. But his mindset was already clear. Thompson said his friend's real dilemma was confronting this question:

> ...whether to float with the tide, or to swim for a goal. It is a choice we must all make consciously or unconsciously at one time in our lives. So few people understand this! Think of any decision you've ever made which had a bearing on your future: I may be wrong, but I don't see how it could have been anything but a choice however indirect—between the two things I've mentioned: the floating or the swimming.[1]

This book is about your choice to float or swim in life, at work, and everywhere else. It's a defining feature of every decision you'll ever make. Thompson's friend was worried about finding his path in life. It's a question we all confront at some point. If you choose a conventional destination, you just need to keep your head above water since the tide is going there anyway. Swimming in any other direction means refusing to let the current decide where you go. It applies in every other context too.

Whether to stay in a familiar but unsatisfying career or make a move.

Whether to remain in a comfortable but unfulfilling relationship or end it.

Whether to lead with a business-as-usual playbook or disrupt it.

Whether to shut up or speak up against the majority.

Whether to cling to old beliefs or question them.

Whether to conform to the status quo or defy it.

These are decisions we make every day in areas big or small. The following chapters will help you make sense of these choices and decide on your course. But it's probably not a book for you.

Almost everyone I've discussed this idea with agrees we should challenge our status quo more often. Yet almost no one does.

I've realized most people want a grander version of conventional success. They want to swim faster and farther in a familiar direction. And there's nothing wrong with making that choice. Many people are perfectly satisfied doing exactly that. But that's not what this book is about.

It is for those who want to live life on their own terms but fail to make it happen. Those who want to lead change but end up following the crowd. Those who feel like they haven't chosen their path. Who feel they're settling instead of thriving. The minority of people who want to break with their status quo but are stuck. It is for the aspiring nonconformists who want to swim like their lives depend on it but don't know where to start.

If this isn't you, this is where we say goodbye. But before you go, here's a parting thought from the end of Thompson's letter:

> No one HAS to do something he doesn't want to do for the rest of his life. But then again, if that's what you wind up doing, by all means convince yourself that you HAD to do it. You'll have lots of company.[2]

CONFORMITY'S HIDDEN COST

To live life on your terms, to truly swim against the tide, you're up against our universal tendency to conform. Or, more accurately, to *mindlessly* conform to your past behaviors, social influences, and the world around you.

Conformity can be rational or ridiculous. Think about how we encourage it in children but mock it in cults. Or how we maintain good habits and struggle to break bad ones. And how some traditions have "stood the test of time" while others persist despite being outdated.

Psychologist Steve Stewart-Williams offers this argument in favor of conformity:

> It's often a good idea to adopt the practices and beliefs of the people around you. For one thing, the people around you aren't dead. If you do what they do—eat what they eat; avoid the dark alleys they avoid—you might continue not being dead as well.[3]

I like the idea of continuing not to be dead. So sticking with what's tried and true is rational when the risks of a wrong decision are costly and irreversible.

We also face an overwhelming number of choices every day. Life's too short to deliberate on every last one. The status quo is a helpful shortcut in low-stakes decisions. A few years ago, I had lunch with friends at a new restaurant. While most of us took time to study the menu, one friend quickly made a choice. He figured it was unlikely to be his last meal, so going with something familiar was good enough. This applies to many of our choices. There's no need to overthink trivial choices. We're better off using our limited mental energy for more important decisions.

The most obvious reason to be a conformist is if the status quo can't be improved. There's no point in fixing what isn't broken. If you're happily married, there's little to be gained and lots to be lost by "exploring your options."

There are other reasons to float along safely with the tide, but there are other places to mention them.

The problem, as you'll learn, is we're not selective in our conformity. We conform even when, as comedian George Carlin once said, "The status quo sucks."[4]

Many of us notice parts of the issue: we're stuck in a comfort zone, we follow social influence, we're creatures of habit, and we suffer from cognitive biases.

What's not so simple is seeing the theme here. All our behavior and beliefs gravitate toward the status quo. This occurs without our awareness, in every domain of life, and often against our best interests.

This default approach to life is what I call the Conformity Coma: *our widespread, unconscious attachment to the status quo that prevents us from making beneficial changes in ourselves and the world around us.*

Part I of this book exposes this tendency so you can recognize it in yourself and others. While conformity typically refers to our tendency to follow the social influence of others, my usage here is broader. I describe how we conform in three parts. These conformity traps cover the variety of status quo influences that affect us. They are:

1. **The trap of consistency:** Persisting with behaviors and beliefs long after they've stopped working or making sense
2. **The trap of compliance:** Letting the opinions and expectations of others shape choices, even when they clash with personal truth or objective reality
3. **The trap of complacency:** Accepting the world as it is without question, missing opportunities for positive change

These traps result in our floating toward mediocrity in important parts of our lives. Tragically, we often realize this too late.

Australian palliative-care nurse, Bronnie Ware, spent years with patients in their final weeks, collecting their reflections on life's regrets. The one she heard most often was that people wished they'd had the courage to live true to themselves instead of conforming to others' expectations. Many realized too late how many dreams they had left unfulfilled.[5]

What these patients regretted most was following a path of conformity instead of rejecting it to pursue their dreams. In his book *Who Not How*, Dan Sullivan puts this idea starkly: "Someone once told me the definition of Hell: The last day you have on earth, the person you became will meet the person you could have become."[6]

This Regret at the end of life, with a capital R, is really the summation of many regrets that pile up over a lifetime:

- Making major life decisions based on what's familiar, acceptable, and conventional.
- Not speaking your mind or standing up for what you believe in.
- Not taking the risks to impact the world around you.

No one wants to be a passive spectator in their life. We want to be the leading actors and choose our roles, regardless of where we're starting from. But unless we take control of our bias to conform, we're living in a game with one rule: your status quo determines your life.

For some, this is literally true. Prisoners, refugees fleeing conflict or persecution, and those living in authoritarian regimes are constrained by external forces that restrict their ability to make independent decisions.

This book focuses on a different problem: how we limit our freedom through self-imposed but made-up rules. By surrendering to social influence, maintaining beliefs and behaviors, and accepting the world's current state when improvement is possible. Since conformity is our collective baseline, we can only improve our outcomes by hoping for a better status quo or mastering our instincts to conform.

But hoping for better circumstances isn't a strategy. We don't have full control over our status quo influences. We have no control over the forces of luck and serendipity, which explains why we were born to these parents, in this society, at this particular time in a world that is the way it is now. And we can't go back and change our past decisions.

What we can control is our decision to conform or defy, and it's one of the most important decisions you'll ever make.

THERE'S ANOTHER WAY

Conformity traps us in a life we haven't chosen. But there's an alternative to this unconscious drift: a deliberate approach to navigating our choices. There's a lot we can learn from people who chose this defiant path.

Musician Frank Zappa's life was short. But he lived out his fifty-two years on his terms. His music—blending rock, jazz, classical, and experimental sounds—defied conventional genres, with some considering him "the most innovative and stylistically daring musician of his generation."[7] His controversial lyrics challenged social norms, political systems, and mainstream culture. He was outspoken about censorship, mainstream education, and organized religion. Whatever regrets he might have had, it's unlikely that conformity was one of them. In an interview, he once described his approach to music:

> I have a basic mechanical knowledge of the operation of the instrument, and I got an imagination, and when the time comes up in the song to play a solo, it's me against the laws of nature. I don't know what I'm going to play. I don't know what I'm going to do. I know roughly how long I have to do it, and it's a game where you have a piece of time, and you get to decorate it, and depending on how intuitive the rhythm section is that's backing you up, you can do things that are literally impossible to imagine sitting here, but you can see them performed before your very eyes in a live performance situation.[8]

You have a piece of time, and you get to decorate it.

This is such a great line, and it could have been written about life too. We get a piece of time; we know roughly how long we have if we're lucky: seventy to eighty, probably no more than one hundred years. If you decide to, you can do things that are impossible to imagine sitting here today. You get to decorate your piece of time however you want. But only if you don't allow conformity to confine you to playing those familiar tunes.

The alternative path is what I call Rational Defiance: *the deliberate decision to challenge the status quo when it stands in the way of something better.*

I use the word "rational" here to distinguish this approach from an aimless rebellion that seeks disruption for its own sake. This isn't about being different just to stand out. It's about making conscious choices to defy the status quo when doing so leads to better outcomes for yourself and for others. I'm making a case for rebels with a cause.

Rational Defiance is a broad principle. Once you're aware of it, you'll see it everywhere:

In *business,* startups epitomize Rational Defiance when they identify unmet needs and inefficiencies, then build solutions that challenge industry conventions.

In *society*, movements for change begin when people question deeply entrenched norms and injustices.

In *science*, breakthroughs emerge when researchers question established theories and conduct experiments that defy conventional wisdom.

In the *arts*, creative rebels push boundaries and experiment with form, subject, and meaning.

While these examples are often celebrated, Rational Defiance also shows up in quieter, everyday contexts:

In our *personal lives*, transformation begins when we defy societal expectations or break habitual patterns. Whether adopting healthier habits, pursuing an unconventional career, or changing long-standing beliefs, these acts of defiance reflect a commitment to growth over comfort.

In the *workplace*, innovation happens when individuals find unique solutions instead of following standard practices. Their practical defiance improves systems and solves problems others have accepted as inevitable.

In *daily interactions*, speaking up against unfairness or expressing well-reasoned opinions that go against group consensus represents small but significant acts of Rational Defiance.

What connects all these examples is simple: they challenge the status quo not just to be different but to make things better.

At first, many of these acts of defiance appear like magic or the result of individuals who simply "possessed the right qualities." We resist the idea that the spark of inspiration and the fortitude to pursue defiant acts can be studied or learned. I believe that's a mistake.

This book is about how we can create the conditions for this kind of positive defiance. I'm not promising a formula to build a unicorn startup, start a revolution, or paint the next Mona Lisa. I'm also not suggesting you should want any of those things. What I am certain of is that whatever you truly desire, Rational Defiance is what you'll need to get there.

Rational Defiance is foremost a philosophy, a general way of approaching the world and your actions in it. It is a mindset that forms the foundation for defiance and a practical strategy for applying it in your life.

In the chapters ahead, I'll show you how to develop this mindset, create your own philosophy of defiance, and apply specific tactics to break free from the conformity traps. You'll learn how to see clearly, seek radical input, sample unconventional experiences, and stand for something that matters to you. Most importantly, you'll discover how to stay defiant when pressures to conform are strongest.

All of this is worth doing because your piece of time is limited, and how you decorate it will be entirely up to you.

FROM ONE CONFORMIST TO ANOTHER

I didn't write a book on Rational Defiance because I'm a model of the idea. Rather than preaching from the summit, I'm writing from the climb. And that's precisely why my perspective should matter to you.

The clue that set off this journey came from an unexpected place: toothpaste.

While running a research agency, we kept encountering a puzzling pattern in consumer behavior. People would explicitly state they preferred one brand yet consistently purchase another they had bought before. This held true across every category we studied: from toothpaste and soft drinks to medicines and financial services. Even when their preferred brand was affordable and readily available, they remained loyal to the less-preferred brand they had always used.

The pattern was so reliable we could predict what most people would buy simply by looking at what they had bought before. But why would someone keep buying something they didn't prefer? What invisible force kept them loyal to products they didn't even like best?

This question led me to research on status quo bias—our tendency to stick with the current state even when better alternatives exist. What began as a consumer insight gradually transformed into a lens through which I view all human behavior, including my own.

In 2016, I was thirty-two and had built our agency from nothing to a market leader. What began as two people with an idea and no funding had grown over eight years into the largest digital research firm in our market.

For at least a year leading up to that point, I experienced two powerful feelings that were hard to resolve. On the one hand, I had a growing desire to make a change and explore another path. However, I also felt resistance to even consider this. The company was successful, we were growing rapidly, and my identity was linked to building it for most of my adult life. It was familiar and comfortable, so why fix what isn't broken?

When we sold the business two years later, it wasn't because I had recognized my attachment to my status quo. It was only afterward with time to reflect when I saw what I had faced wasn't simply a career decision but a tension between conformity and defiance. I was staring at the same pattern we'd observed in consumers. I was the person sticking with what was familiar even while wanting something different.

This reframing clarified not just my dilemma but a pattern I began to see everywhere: in careers, relationships, organizations, and societies.

When I dug deeper, my search benefited from my background in several ways. My academic background as a PhD in cognitive psychology gave me the tools to explore the science behind this pattern. Years of building a startup taught me firsthand how hard it is to challenge established ways of thinking. And my uneasy relationship with convention—beginning with questioning my childhood beliefs in my early twenties—provided personal insight into what's at stake when we choose to defy or conform.

The more I researched and reflected, the more I realized something striking: very few of us recognize the full extent to which conformity affects us. We might notice pieces—a bad habit here, peer pressure there—but not the complete picture.

This book is the result. It's both a diagnosis of why we remain trapped in conformity and a practical framework for breaking free. It draws from research in psychology, modern and ancient philosophy, alongside case studies of defiant individuals and my observations and experiences.

While the advice is always to write for an audience of one, I realized I was writing for myself. A reminder of what's at stake when we drift through life on autopilot and what to do about it. If you've ever felt that tension between who you are and who you could be, then I'm writing for you too.

WHAT TO EXPECT

This is a short book, one that you can read in a few hours or days. It revolves around the two main ideas I've introduced here.

The first is the *Conformity Coma*: a universal psychological force that traps us without our awareness. In Part I, we'll identify the problem and describe the three hidden traps that keep us stuck in the status quo.

The second is *Rational Defiance*: a deliberate approach to a more authentic path forward. Part II defines the idea and provides the mindset necessary to challenge the status quo. Part III covers the practical strategies for turning this mindset into a defiant path.

I suggest reading the book in this order. Part I matters because we underestimate conformity's grip, and you can't change what you don't recognize. Part II introduces Rational Defiance as the antidote to mindless conformity (not mindless rebellion) and builds the mindset that makes thoughtful defiance possible. Part III shows how to plan sustained defiant action that creates real change.

But don't treat this as a rigid checklist. Rational Defiance isn't a recipe to follow step by step. Apply even a few ideas to select areas of your life, and you'll find yourself on a more authentic, less conformist path.

I want to be clear about what this book isn't: it's not a prescription for any particular version of nonconformity. I won't tell you to quit your job, start a business, move to a remote island, or adopt any specific lifestyle. Rational Defiance isn't about exchanging one formula for another. It's about developing the clarity to recognize when the status quo doesn't serve you and the courage to chart your own course. What that looks like will be uniquely yours, as it should be.

In this short format, I focus on the big ideas and principles. You won't find endless variations of the same ideas or chapter-long anecdotes. That's the trade-off. A shorter book where you play your part. I believe those who would benefit from this book will take this deal. I hope you're one of them.

Part I

The Conformity Coma

IF YOU'RE STILL READING, YOU SUSPECT CONFORMITY IS holding you back. But it's worse than you think. Conformity isn't just peer pressure or a few bad habits. It's everywhere—in how you work, who you spend time with, what you believe, even in dreams you've given up on without realizing it. The next four chapters will show you exactly how this happens. You'll see how you're trapped by your past choices, by what others expect of you, and by accepting "the way things are" without question. This might sting a bit. Nobody likes discovering they have less control over their life than they thought. But until you see it, you can't change it.

CHAPTER ONE

Stuck in the Status Quo

IMAGINE THAT SCIENTISTS CREATE A MACHINE THAT enables you to live your ideal life. You can have any experience you desire, whether it's being a billionaire, creating incredible art, finding love, or achieving fame. Once connected, you'll feel like you're achieving your dreams and living the perfect life. You can plug into this machine for the rest of your life. Once you do, you will forget about the real world and experience only the reality created by the machine.

Would you plug in?

Most of us wouldn't. But why? Robert Nozick, who wrote about this thought experiment in 1974, suggested we don't want to lose contact with reality. He argues we value our real lives, with their ups and downs, over endless artificial pleasures.[9]

But what happens when we reverse the situation? Imagine that you have been living your life in this experience machine until now. Your entire reality has resulted from being connected to a simulation. If you get the chance, would you unplug and return to your "real" life?

Felipe De Brigard conducted an experiment to test this question in 2010. He presented study participants with the scenario that their entire lives had been lived in a machine simulation, and they could now choose to stay in the simulation or leave. To one group, he provided no information about their lives outside the machine (the neutral scenario), another group was told they were prisoners in a maximum-security jail (negative), and a third group was told they were multimillionaire artists living in Monaco (positive).[10] Regardless of the details, if "contact with reality" is so important, we'd expect most people would choose to return to their real lives.

But that's not what happened.

In the negative scenario, almost everyone wanted to stay connected.[11] This is reasonable since they're dodging a prison sentence by staying in the Matrix.

But here's where things get interesting. In the neutral scenario, 46 percent still decided to remain in the experience machine. And even when a pleasant life in Monaco awaited, a full 50 percent chose to stay plugged in.[12] Instead of jumping at the chance to return to their real lives, many decided to stay where they were.

What we're afraid of isn't losing contact with reality but losing our status quo. Whether we're told we can live our ideal lives in a simulation or return to a wonderful life in Monaco, we prefer what we know.

None of us live in a simulation (as far as we know), but we face this same reluctance every day. We want improvement and change, but we hesitate to unplug from our reality. We cling to familiar jobs, relationships, habits, and beliefs, even when better alternatives exist.

This bit of sci-fi psychology is part of a large body of real-world evidence that reveals a similar pattern. Your current reality, what I call your *individual status quo*, is shaped by three powerful forces:

- Your past decisions, beliefs, and behavior.
- The influence of others.
- The prevailing conditions of the world.

These factors create your version of "normal." And when deciding, you're biased toward options that conform to the status quo: options that feel familiar, socially acceptable, and consistent with the world as you know it.

The critical insight is this: *You would make different choices if you weren't exposed to these status quo influences.* Your decisions aren't freely made; they're heavily filtered through the lens of what already exists.

This pattern appears repeatedly in research findings and real-world examples. Let's look at the evidence.

THE EVIDENCE

In a landmark 1988 paper, economists William Samuelson and Richard Zeckhauser coined the term "status quo bias" to describe our tendency to prefer things as they are, even when change would benefit us.[13]

One of their experiments illustrated this effect using financial decision-making. Participants were told they had inherited a large sum from a deceased great-uncle and were asked to decide how to invest it. They were given four investment options with varying risk profiles, expected returns, and asset classes.[14]

One group of participants had to make a decision with no prior investment, effectively starting from scratch.[15]

Another group was told their uncle had already invested the money into one of the four options, and they could either leave it as is or switch to another investment.[16]

The results were striking: when an existing investment was already in place, participants overwhelmingly preferred to stick with it. Even more fascinating, which specific investment was presented as the status quo didn't matter. Participants consistently favored whichever option was framed as the existing choice.[17]

This reveals something fundamental about decision-making: the mere presence of a status quo option significantly changes our preferences. We don't choose what's best. We choose what's already there.

This pattern extends far beyond laboratory experiments. It shapes economies, public policy, and personal lives in ways both subtle and profound.

Take Google's dominance in search. In 2023, court documents from Google's antitrust trial revealed that the company paid a staggering $26.3 billion in 2021 alone to remain the default search engine on various platforms, including Apple and Android devices. Why such an astronomical sum? Because Google understands that most users will stick with the default rather than change it, even when equally good alternatives are just a few clicks away.

Subscription-based businesses like Netflix, Spotify, and countless software-as-a-service (SaaS) companies have built their business models around this same bias. By structuring their services with automatic renewals rather than requiring active resubscription, they ensure that customers will default to staying subscribed. When users must opt-in to continue a service, renewal rates drop dramatically; when they're automatically renewed, most continue paying without a second thought.

This effect is so powerful that regulatory bodies have started requiring "cancel anytime" options and pre-expiry notifications to prevent businesses from unfairly exploiting user inertia.

Another consequential example comes from organ donation policies around the world. Some countries, like the United States and the United Kingdom, use an opt-in system where individuals must actively register to become donors. Others, such as France and Austria, employ an opt-out system where everyone is automatically registered unless they explicitly choose otherwise.

The difference in donation rates is profound: in opt-in countries, donation rates hover around 15 percent on average, while opt-out countries consistently see rates exceeding 90 percent.[18] The default policy literally decides if thousands of lives are saved or lost each year, not due to deeply held values or beliefs but simply because people accept the status quo.

We see the same pattern in our careers and personal lives. A 2024 Gallup poll found that US employee engagement reached an eleven-year low, yet employee quit rates did not increase.[19] Despite widespread dissatisfaction, most people remain in place, accepting the devil they know over the uncertainty of change.

The chapters that follow contain many more examples of how deeply we're plugged into our status quo, including how:

- Habits, not conscious choices, drive most of our daily behaviors.
- We change our opinions based on social influence even when objective facts contradict the group's view.
- We become more accepting of controversial ideas when told they have a long history.
- We defend systems that harm us simply because they're familiar.

What Samuelson and Zeckhauser termed "status quo bias" is part of a broader pattern. Researchers across psychology, economics, and sociology have identified various behavioral tendencies that all point to the same conclusion: we're profoundly attached to the status quo. Whether through habit, social conformity, or simple inertia, we always favor what is over what could be.

In psychology, *conformity* refers to changing our beliefs and behaviors to match those around us. However, I use the term more broadly in this book to describe our tendency to align with any status quo influence, whether it's our past behaviors, social pressures, or environmental defaults. When we conform to the status quo, we become more like our past selves, our social groups, and the world around us.

The research evidence is clear and compelling, and the following chapters explore the science behind it. But let's start by considering how much of this we can recognize by observing ourselves and others.

CONFORMITY EVERYWHERE

Conformity's influence is visible everywhere: from morning routines to life-defining choices, from trivial opinions to deeply held beliefs.

Consider a typical day for most working people:

Wake up at six. Check phones. Coffee. Shower. Breakfast. Commute. Work through emails and meetings. Lunch at the same café. More work. Drive home. Dinner. Netflix. Bed.

The specifics differ—some work remotely, prefer sandwiches to salads, or follow different schedules—but most people live on repeat, cycling through personal variations of the same daily routine. People rarely question these patterns. They're simply "what we do." These habits represent a preference for repeating past decisions rather than actively deciding every day.

This same pattern extends to longer timescales too. People remain loyal to projects long after they've stopped yielding results. They stay in relationships that no longer fulfill them because they're familiar. They pursue career paths chosen by versions of themselves that no longer exist. Consider how this works: An eighteen-year-old version of someone chooses their career path. Their twenty-something self fell in love and committed to a partner. A slightly more recent version took on projects or commitments that now feel like burdens. These past decisions follow people through life, influencing their present even when circumstances have changed dramatically.

At the grandest scale, conformity shapes entire lives. For generations, the dominant "life script" in Western societies dictated that people study hard, build careers, marry, buy houses, have children, and retire at sixty-five. While these scripts have evolved (perhaps now becoming digital nomads, launching startups, or choosing child-free lifestyles), they still function as powerful templates that shape expectations and choices.

In professional settings, conformity manifests as resistance to new ideas and technologies. Companies stick with outdated processes because "that's how we've always done things." Teams follow familiar playbooks even when they stop working. Employees avoid proposing innovative solutions for fear of rocking the boat. The result is stagnation, a mediocre version of business-as-usual that persists not because it's effective but because it's familiar.

Conformity doesn't just influence what people do; it dictates what they think. Most beliefs aren't developed through careful, independent reasoning. They're inherited from parents, absorbed from peers, or adopted from a broader culture. These borrowed ideas about politics, religion, success, relationships, and countless other domains form the foundation of worldviews, yet they're rarely updated.

Once established, these beliefs function as filters that determine what information gets accepted or rejected. People gravitate toward sources and communities that reinforce existing views while dismissing contradictory evidence. This creates a self-reinforcing cycle: beliefs shape perception, and perception reinforces beliefs.

No domain or demographic escapes conformity. It affects liberals and conservatives, young and old, educated and uneducated alike. It shapes personal habits, professional decisions, and societal structures with equal force.

While these patterns of conformity are evident everywhere, there's one place we're far less likely to notice them.

YES, YOU TOO

It's easy to agree with all of this until we have to ask the question of ourselves. Being aware of a problem doesn't mean you are self-aware. The hardest part is recognizing conformity in yourself.

It's easy to see the mindless conformity of past generations. History is filled with once-accepted beliefs and behaviors that now seem absurd. Slavery persisted for centuries, child labor was routine during the Industrial Revolution, and smoking was glamorized in the mid-twentieth century. Even more recently, it's obvious how norms shift constantly: not long ago, we all worked from the office and wore baggy nineties fashion.

Thoreau, writing in 1854, reminds us how hypocritical this is when he said, "Every generation laughs at the old fashions, but follows religiously the new."[20] We're blind to the status quo we live in, just as past generations were to theirs. Princeton Professor Robert P. George illustrates this with a question he asks of his students: Would you have opposed slavery had you lived in the South pre-abolition? Most say yes, but history suggests otherwise. Few resist prevailing norms, then or now.

You don't need a time machine to view conformity in action; it's all around you. The friend who married young because it was "time," the colleague addicted to emails yet unproductive, or the person who clings to outdated ideas despite contrary evidence.

It's easy to notice conformity from a comfortable distance. What about you? Do you challenge norms, take risks, and live by your own rules? Perhaps, but only sometimes.

Conformity isn't easy to switch off. While we celebrate our infrequent acts of defiance, we conform in other aspects of our lives. Only by observing our past selves objectively can we see our personal history of conformity.

Because our past selves also feel like someone else who had that bad habit; how did we not recognize it for what it was? Someone who made poor decisions based on peer pressure. Someone who believed that a juice cleanse was a sustainable diet, that skinny jeans fit us perfectly, and that politicians are honest. Someone who took the acceptable path instead of the one they desired. With the clarity of hindsight, we see our past selves for what we were: devout conformists.

And then there's you today. Have you ever thought:
That your passions and commitments aren't aligned.
That you're chasing someone else's goals.
That you're living someone else's dream.
That you keep your opinions to yourself.
That you're settling instead of thriving.
That every day is the same as the last.
That decisions are made for you.
That you avoid taking risks.
That you never ask "why."
That you're stuck.

Many of us hear these voices, but they become white noise in the background. We fail to see that these feelings are signs of being stuck in conformity. We don't recognize the real enemy disguised as discomfort.

It's a hidden problem, unlike other areas of self-development. If we know we'd like to improve our health, finances, or relationships, we need a plan. Even if the plan fails, at least we know what needs to change. In the foreword to Katy Milkman's book *How to Change*, Angela Duckworth writes that the book answers the question: "Why is it so very hard to get from where I am to where I want to be?"[21] Because we're ignorant of our conformity, we never ask this question.

John Steinbeck wrote about getting lost on a road trip and pulling out a map to find direction, only to realize that "to find where you are going, you must know where you are, and I didn't."[22] So it's time to admit where you are. Conformity isn't other people's problem. It's yours too. You are a conformist, for better or worse.

Once you recognize this, it becomes easier to face the challenge of conformity. When you do, a deeper question emerges: What connects all these patterns? What invisible force keeps us tethered to our status quo, even when better alternatives exist?

THE CONFORMITY COMA

Economists call it status quo bias. Social scientists study compliance. Psychologists explore the pull of habits. Philosophers question why we accept the world as it is.

These seem like separate issues. But they're different angles on the same fundamental pattern that I call the Conformity Coma: *a widespread, unconscious attachment to the status quo that prevents us from making beneficial changes in ourselves and the world around us.*

It has four defining characteristics:

1. **Maintaining the status quo:** We stick to what's familiar, acceptable, and consistent to avoid change.
2. **Running on autopilot:** We choose the status quo unconsciously.
3. **No intention to improve:** We don't consider whether our choices lead to an improvement.
4. **Always on:** It's our constant baseline state in every area of life.

In isolation, issues such as habits, biases, and social influence seem like adversaries we face in particular parts of our lives. But that's like observing falling apples, ocean tides, and planetary orbits without recognizing they're all governed by the same force of gravity. Similarly, our specific tendencies to favor the status quo, when taken together, are something entirely different: a pervasive state of unconscious conformity that directs our lives on autopilot.

I realize introducing yet another term risks adding to the already cluttered list of self-help jargon. The world hardly needs another catchy phrase to dress up something obvious.

However, the existing vocabulary falls short. None of the existing ideas captures the full spectrum of our unconscious attachment to the familiar. None addresses how these tendencies work together to keep us comfortably numb to possibilities for change. And without naming this unified phenomenon, we struggle to recognize it in ourselves or discuss it meaningfully with others.

It's important to understand that the Conformity Coma isn't about individual decisions made in conformity. It's not about any single habit, bias, or instance of social compliance. It's a pervasive state of being. A default mode of existence that shapes our entire approach to life. Just as a coma is not a single symptom but a profound state of unconsciousness, the Conformity Coma describes our ignorance of the status quo's influence across all domains of our lives.

This is why understanding the Conformity Coma matters. It's the foundation for practical change and the key to examining the three specific traps that maintain it: consistency, compliance, and complacency. The chapters ahead look at these in more detail.

But what's important now is to recognize what they represent: an unconscious preference to avoid change, with no thought to improve, that follows us everywhere. Because you can't wake up if you don't know you're asleep.

OLD PROBLEM, NEW PRESSURES

In one sense, our persistent ignorance of conformity is surprising. While the concept of the Conformity Coma is my own, its features have been recognized for ages. Nathaniel Branden in *Six Pillars of Self-Esteem* observed that

> in virtually all of the great spiritual and philosophical traditions of the world there appears some form of the idea that most human beings are sleepwalking through their own existence...If we do not bring an appropriate level of consciousness to our activities, if we do not live mindfully, the inevitable penalty is a diminished sense of self-efficacy and self-respect.[23]

It's an understanding that spans cultures and centuries. Throughout history, thinkers have warned us about our unconscious conformity to habit and custom. Blaise Pascal observed in the seventeenth century, "Custom is our nature...What are our natural principles but principles of custom?"[24] A few centuries later, William James reached a similar conclusion when he determined that our lives are "bundles of habits."[25]

Philosophers have been equally vocal about our tendency to mindlessly follow social influence. In the fourth century BCE, Diogenes of Sinope, often accused of madness for his eccentric ways, insisted that he was not insane but living according to reason.[26] Twenty-one centuries later, Rousseau echoed this sentiment when writing about society's rules, "Man is born free; and everywhere he is in chains."[27] Oscar Wilde put it more bluntly, "Most people are other people. Their thoughts are someone else's opinions, their lives a mimicry, their passions a quotation."[28]

Even when we recognize the need for change, resistance feels overwhelming. As Machiavelli noted in the sixteenth century: "It must be considered that there is nothing more difficult to carry out, nor more doubtful of success, nor more dangerous to handle, than to initiate a new order of things."[29]

Despite centuries of warnings, Emerson's observation remains true: most people "grow up and grow old in seeming and following."[30]

Yet, in many ways, it's harder to break free from conformity today.

Social influence has intensified dramatically. People now spend an average of 6 hours and 40 minutes in front of screens per day.[31] Back in 1947, Dorothy Sayers observed how, with the arrival of film and radio, people were poorly equipped to handle the "incessant battery of words, words, words."[32] Today, those words have multiplied into tweets, videos, and memes, shaping our thoughts and behaviors at an unprecedented scale. We are constantly nudged to buy the latest gadget or reject consumerism, to #hustle or embrace antihustle culture, to join a movement, or criticize it for being performative.

What's also changed is we have more deeply embedded institutions that promote conformity than ever. Modern schools, by their very nature, encourage conformity. They reward obedience, sort children by age over ability, enforce rigid schedules, and value standardized answers over independent thought. This continues seamlessly into the workplace, where managers replace teachers, standardized tasks replace tests, and dress codes replace school uniforms. We spend more of our lives caught within these structures than ever.

Organizations and governments further exploit our preference for the familiar through "default nudging" by designing choices so people unconsciously accept the path of least resistance. Often under the guise of promoting well-being but sometimes for more self-serving ends. As our understanding of our biases grew, so did the power to use these against us.

Amid all this, there has been a rise in fake versions of nonconformity, which need to be recognized for what they are. In some circles, being a "nonconformist" has become fashionable. But mindlessly following a smaller crowd isn't independent thinking. Just because a movement claims to have risen against the status quo doesn't mean it's on to something.

Our mental wiring, evolved for small, tight-knit groups, is ill-equipped for today's relentless social pressures and institutional influences. Whatever benefits conformity once had in simpler societies, it now works against us in an era where powerful systems and constant information overload shape our choices without our awareness. Recognizing these forces and resisting them is more important than ever.

THE CONFORMITY TRAPS

The Conformity Coma describes our overall pattern of unconscious attachment to the status quo. However, to recognize and overcome this pattern in your life, you need to know exactly where to look.

Our tendency toward conformity appears in three distinct contexts. These "conformity traps" are invisible, deceptive, and often harmful.

Like a physical trap that is hidden or disguised, psychological traps are not immediately apparent. They create the illusion we're on the best path when we're not. When we fall for them, we justify our actions with standard ideas of why we behave this way.

The three traps are:

1. **The trap of consistency:** Persisting with behaviors and beliefs long after they've stopped working or making sense
2. **The trap of compliance:** Letting others' opinions and expectations shape our choices, even when they clash with our personal truth or objective reality
3. **The trap of complacency:** Accepting the world as it is without question and missing opportunities for positive change

Each trap represents a different way we conform: to our past selves, to other people, and to our environment. In the chapters ahead, I'll dive into each of these traps. I'll show you how they work and how they might play out in your life right now.

First, we'll look at why consistency, usually seen as a virtue, may frequently be a vice.

CHAPTER TWO

The Consistency Trap

IN 2020, FACEBOOK ANNOUNCED A FEATURE THAT allowed users to delete their old posts:

> Whether you're entering the job market after college or moving on from an old relationship, we know things change in people's lives, and we want to make it easy for you to curate your presence on Facebook to more accurately reflect who you are today.

It's obvious why people want to curate their digital past. Nobody wants that embarrassing photo from 2011 or that politically charged rant from 2016 to define them forever. We don't want a past version of ourselves parading around in the future.

Yet, outside of Facebook, our past is harder to shake. We allow outdated beliefs, past decisions, and habitual actions to shape our lives today.

It's true that persistence can be beneficial. Repeating behaviors as unconscious routines helps us avoid the countless decisions we'd have to make anew every day. Persisting despite challenges helps us achieve meaningful goals. Standing firm in our convictions when facing pressure to conform is admirable.

But blind persistence is often our downfall. We continue failing pursuits long after they should be abandoned. We cling to outdated beliefs despite contradicting evidence. We mindlessly repeat unproductive habits that no longer align with who we want to become.

This is the trap of consistency: *persisting with behaviors and beliefs long after they've stopped working or making sense.*

The embarrassing 2010 version of you may be hidden on Facebook, but your past self still directs your life in invisible ways. In this chapter, we'll look at the problem from two angles. We'll explore our tendency to persist in our actions and examine how we maintain mental consistency by clinging to long-held beliefs.

By understanding these patterns, you'll learn to distinguish between beneficial persistence that helps you achieve goals and the kind that traps you in outdated patterns.

ACTIONS WE REPEAT

Whether it's the athlete who never misses a workout or the professional who stays with one company for decades, we view persistence as an example of discipline and dependability.

Take action, stick with it, and succeed. Or so the story goes.

The evidence shows a different picture: we often stick to our actions for too long, against our best interests. We do this in two ways.

First, our daily behaviors are dominated by habits, automated routines triggered by familiar cues that unfold with minimal awareness. These can propel us toward success but often trap us in cycles we don't even notice.

Second, we remain committed to paths long after evidence suggests we should change course. Careers we've invested years in, relationships we've nurtured, projects we've poured resources into. Our reluctance to walk away keeps us chained to past decisions.

Psychological mechanisms anchor our consistency, causing us to repeat actions even when they no longer make sense. Like a ship following outdated navigation charts, we continue along familiar routes rather than plotting a new course toward our true destination.

DAILY AUTOPILOT

What's the first thing you do every morning? If you're like millions of others, you reach for your smartphone before you're fully awake. No conscious decision drives this action. Your hand moves automatically, responding to a trigger you don't even register.

Our lives are filled with these automated behaviors. William James observed over a century ago, "Ninety-nine hundredths or, possibly, nine hundred and ninety-nine thousandths of our activity is purely automatic and habitual."[33] The latest research puts this figure closer to 40 percent, still a remarkable number of actions taken on autopilot.[34]

This isn't necessarily a problem. Habits are the brain's efficiency system. They free up mental bandwidth by turning recurring decisions into automatic routines. Each habit develops through a three-part loop:

First comes the **cue**: *a trigger that signals the brain to activate a routine.* This could be a time of day, an emotional state, a location, or the presence of certain people.

Next is the **routine**: *the behavior itself, whether physical, mental, or emotional.*

Finally, the **reward**: *the benefit that reinforces the habit, making you more likely to repeat it in the future.*

When aligned with our goals, this system is remarkably powerful. The executive who automatically reaches for running shoes each morning doesn't debate whether to exercise; she just does it. The writer who sits down at the same time each day doesn't wait for inspiration; words flow because the habit has been established. These positive routines create success with minimal willpower.

But the same mechanism works against us when habits form without intention or outlive their usefulness. The smartphone habit that began as an efficient way to check important messages becomes mindless scrolling that consumes hours. The occasional drink to unwind after work transitions imperceptibly into a nightly requirement. The defensive communication pattern that protected you in one relationship sabotages all future ones.

What makes these negative habits particularly dangerous is our blindness to them. Consider a study where researchers gave people either fresh or stale popcorn at a movie theater. Those without a "popcorn habit" ate less of the stale popcorn, as you might expect. But habitual popcorn eaters consumed the same amount regardless of quality. Their behavior had become disconnected from the experience.

This same disconnection explains many stubborn patterns in our lives. The manager who micromanages their team doesn't see how this undermines their growth and their own strategic focus. The person who habitually delays important decisions doesn't recognize how this temporary relief creates larger problems. The professional who checks email first thing every morning doesn't realize how this reactive start hijacks their entire day.

We don't explicitly choose these patterns; they form through repetition and become our default operating system. Once established, they run in the background of our lives, directing our actions while evading our awareness.

This is how habits become a consistency trap. They represent the past programming itself into our present, regardless of whether that programming still serves us. Breaking free requires recognizing these invisible patterns. The routines that have become so familiar we no longer question them, even as the world changes and our goals evolve.

DOUBLING DOWN ON FAILURE

Habits explain why we repeat our past behavior. Another set of tendencies explains why we stick to our past decisions, even when they're clearly failing.

We all know we need to persevere to reach our goals. Great success stories often follow the same storyline: The hero starts on an uncertain journey with a great reward. They overcome countless obstacles through dedication and perseverance, culminating in their triumph. This quality, which Angela Duckworth describes as "grit" in her book by the same name, is why we admire those who reach success in sport, business, and life. It's why we have sayings like "Winners never quit, and quitters never win."

But what about situations where quitting is the wiser choice? As Warren Buffett put it, "Should you find yourself in a chronically leaking boat, energy devoted to changing vessels is likely to be more productive than energy devoted to patching leaks."[35]

Two psychological tendencies make it hard to change course in the face of failure: the sunk-cost fallacy and escalation of commitment.

The sunk-cost fallacy occurs when we persist with a decision simply because we've already invested in it. In a 1985 study, psychologists Hal Arkes and Catherine Blumer described a scenario where participants accidentally bought tickets for two ski trips on the same weekend—one twice as expensive as the other, even though they expected to enjoy the cheaper trip more. When asked which trip they would take, most chose the costlier option, illustrating the sunk-cost fallacy. (In the original study, the tickets cost $100 and $50 respectively—about $300 and $150 in today's terms.)[36]

The sensible answer is you should go on the Wisconsin ski trip since that is what you prefer. You've already paid the costs for the more expensive Michigan trip, but you can't be refunded. However, the study's results showed that only 46 percent chose the Wisconsin trip despite thinking it would be more enjoyable.[37] The higher sunk costs for the Michigan trip bound them to a less enjoyable destination.

The sunk-cost fallacy is closely related to the escalation of commitment, which leads us to keep investing in a past decision despite evidence that it is failing. A famous real-life example has become known as the Concorde fallacy. In 1956, the French and British governments and engine manufacturers decided to build a supersonic plane, the Concorde. The budget was estimated at $100 million. Yet long before the project was completed, it was clear it would never be profitable. However, the project continued with further investments because of the massive costs already incurred. Ultimately, the Concorde operated for less than thirty years, leading to millions in wasted investment. It's an example that lives on as an extreme case of throwing good money after bad.

Most of us have faced the situation of being committed to a losing course of action. There are many reasons people stay in unhappy relationships. But the sunk cost and escalation biases explain many of these cases. After spending years with someone, we're reluctant to consider this time and emotional investment as wasted. The same is true for careers we've outgrown. After so much time and effort, surely we're better off staying in this job than risking a change. With so much money and training spent on a new piece of software that doesn't tick all the boxes, we still feel we need to see it through. It's why so many companies keep supporting failing projects long after it was clear they should abandon their plans.

Persevering despite obstacles is a necessary skill, but so is knowing when to quit. Sometimes, we're dealt a losing hand, and the real wisdom lies in recognizing when to press on and when to walk away.

BELIEFS WE KEEP

Psychological insights also explain why it's hard to change our minds. We often see this as a virtue; we admire those who stand firm in their beliefs, viewing them as reliable and trustworthy. Think of how you react when a politician reverses their stance or when a leader frequently changes direction.

Of course, we value this consistency only when the original beliefs are accurate and when they solve problems, provide motivation, and allow us to act with integrity.

The problem is that the strength of our convictions is rarely proportionate to the degree to which they have these positive qualities. Our mental consistency is rooted in several biases that make us cling to beliefs despite good reasons to abandon them. A quote often attributed to writer Rober Breault puts it this way: "An old belief is like an old shoe. We so value its comfort that we fail to notice the hole in it."

A combination of cognitive dissonance and confirmation bias makes us stubbornly cling to our old ideas. Like an old but comfortable shoe, we avoid upgrading and instead constantly patch the holes in them.

WHEN FACTS DON'T FIT

Cognitive dissonance occurs when we hold two contradictory beliefs at once. Instead of abandoning the old idea, we often double down.

The concept was introduced in the 1956 work *When Prophecy Fails* by Leon Festinger, Henry Riecken, and Stanley Schachter. The book documented their time with the Seekers, a Midwestern doomsday cult led by Dorothy Martin, who claimed extraterrestrials had warned her of a catastrophic flood that would occur on December 21, 1954. The group sold their possessions and cut ties with nonbelievers, expecting to be rescued by a flying saucer.[38]

When the prophecy failed, the group didn't admit they were wrong. Instead, they rationalized the event, believing their faith had prevented the disaster. Festinger and his colleagues explained this behavior: when deeply held beliefs are contradicted by reality, people justify and reinterpret facts rather than change their views. They refused to let the truth spoil the story they had told themselves.[39]

While most people aren't part of UFO cults, cognitive dissonance affects everyone, including supposedly rational professionals. One of history's most striking examples comes from medicine.

In the nineteenth century, Hungarian physician Ignaz Semmelweis noticed that maternal mortality rates at Vienna General Hospital were significantly higher in a clinic where doctors performed autopsies before assisting births. He hypothesized that "cadaverous particles" were infecting mothers and implemented a hand-washing protocol, which reduced deaths from childbed fever to under 2 percent.[40]

Despite clear evidence, the medical community rejected Semmelweis's findings. His idea challenged established norms, and instead of updating their beliefs, doctors resisted change. It wasn't until Louis Pasteur and Joseph Lister advanced germ theory decades later that hand hygiene became standard practice. Semmelweis never received credit and died in an asylum in 1865.[41] His story is a striking example of scientific cognitive dissonance, now known as the Semmelweis reflex, the tendency to reject new ideas that contradict prevailing beliefs.

Cognitive dissonance is everywhere. Many pursue corporate careers believing success is defined by climbing the ladder. But over time, conflicting values, such as a desire for independence, fulfillment, or work-life balance, create dissonance. Instead of reassessing their definition of success, some justify staying on the same path.

The same occurs in relationships. Many believe being unmarried at a "certain age" signals failure, even as they acknowledge relationships should be about compatibility and not social expectations.

Others value healthy eating but indulge frequently, or believe in evidence-based thinking but follow the online consensus of unqualified strangers, and many claim to prefer real-life interactions but spend most of their time on social media.

When confronted with contradictions, we either change our beliefs or rationalize them to maintain the status quo. More often than not, we choose the latter.

PROVING OURSELVES RIGHT

When confronted with new information that challenges our beliefs, we instinctively reject it to reduce cognitive dissonance. We also seek out and favor information that confirms what we already believe. This is confirmation bias, a tendency observed for centuries. In 1620, Francis Bacon wrote:

> The human understanding, when any proposition has been once laid down (either from general admission and belief, or from the pleasure it affords), forces everything else to add fresh support and confirmation; and although most cogent and abundant instances may exist to the contrary, yet either does not observe or despises them, or gets rid of and rejects them by some distinction, with violent and injurious prejudice, rather than sacrifice the authority of its first conclusions.[42]

Modern research has repeatedly confirmed this effect. A 1979 study on the death penalty showed participants two fabricated studies: one supporting and one refuting its effectiveness. Regardless of the evidence, participants found the study supporting their preexisting view more convincing and became even more entrenched.[43]

A 2023 study on vaccine efficacy revealed the same pattern. Both pro- and antivaccine participants made systematic errors when evaluating data that contradicted their prior beliefs. Instead of weighing the evidence objectively, they interpreted it in ways that aligned with their stance.[44]

Today, confirmation bias is amplified by the information landscape. Political views are among the strongest beliefs we hold, and media outlets often cater to partisan audiences rather than presenting neutral facts. Instead of challenging our biases, they reinforce them.

On the internet, a single Google search can confirm any belief, no matter how unfounded. On social media, we hang out in groups with the same views. The web's "filter bubble" algorithms reinforce our one-sidedness by prioritizing exposure to the content we have engaged with before. The result of all of this is an information echo chamber that reinforces our views. Our selective information diets are unbalanced but psychologically satisfying.

But as Will Self observes in a 2016 article in *The New Statesmen*, "The real filter bubble is you."[45] What drives our filtered view of the world is not the media that provides sources that support our views but our tendency to avoid cognitive dissonance and seek confirming evidence for our beliefs in the first place. The media simply provided the tools for our biases to run free.

This is true in every area and for everyone. Jurors may favor evidence that aligns with their preconceptions while ignoring contradictory testimony. Superstitions persist because we remember when they seem to work but forget when they don't. Investors often ignore warnings that contradict their market outlook, leading to costly mistakes. Scientists may unconsciously favor data that confirms their hypothesis while dismissing contradictory results. Relationships suffer when we interpret a partner's actions through the lens of past assumptions rather than objectively assessing them. Sports fans selectively recall their team's wins while excusing losses. Historians may interpret events through cultural or ideological biases rather than examining all perspectives.

On Substack, biologist Richard Dawkins wrote about what he calls "the evidence-based life" and how easy it is for us to be trapped by our thought biases. He asks us to consider the strength of our opinions:

Have I looked even-handedly at the available evidence or did I under-value or even ignore evidence that contradicted my prior beliefs?...Do I read only the *Guardian* and ignore the *Telegraph*? Or vice versa. Do I watch only Fox News and ignore CNN? Do I tune out when exposed to news, or views, that contradict my prior prejudices?[46]

We don't ask ourselves these kinds of questions because we rarely evaluate our beliefs. Once we've adopted them, we stay consistent, ignoring all evidence to the contrary.

CURATED CONSISTENCY

Writing in 1841, Ralph Waldo Emerson had little respect for those who place a high value on consistency above all else:

> A foolish consistency is the hobgoblin of little minds, adored by little statesmen and philosophers and divines. With consistency a great soul has simply nothing to do. He may as well concern himself with his shadow on the wall.[47]

Emerson wrote these words in his essay "Self-Reliance," a manifesto for independent thinking and personal authenticity. He wasn't dismissing all forms of consistency. After all, he championed living by one's deepest principles. What he rejected was consistency for its own sake: clinging to past statements or positions to avoid the appearance of contradiction.

For Emerson, genuine growth required the courage to evolve beyond previous versions of yourself. The truly self-reliant person isn't afraid to contradict their former self when new understanding emerges. As he wrote elsewhere in the same essay, "Speak what you think now in hard words and to-morrow speak what to-morrow thinks in hard words again, though it contradict every thing you said to-day."[48]

This distinction between principled persistence and "foolish consistency" is precisely what we need to understand.

Surprisingly, Facebook's new feature provides a model for how this should be done. The company used the word "curate" to describe its feature for hiding old posts. I think this form of curation is the right way to approach our real-world relationship with the past too. Instead of allowing the past to dictate our future, we can select those parts we want to let live on. Being consistent in our beliefs and behaviors that continue to serve us well is not incompatible with changing our minds and actions to better reflect who we are today.

CHAPTER THREE

The Compliance Trap

IN 1966, A TEAM OF RESEARCHERS CONDUCTED A DISTURBing experiment in a Midwestern hospital. An unknown "doctor" phoned the nurses on duty, instructing them to administer 20 mg of a drug called Astroten to specific patients. The order violated hospital policy in three ways: the dosage was twice the maximum indicated on the medication label, the order came by telephone from a doctor the nurses had never met, and hospital rules required written authorization before dispensing the medication.[49]

Yet despite these clear violations, twenty-one out of twenty-two nurses prepared the excessive dose.[50] They were stopped only when the researchers intervened. These weren't incompetent or unethical nurses, but trained professionals who knew the rules. Yet they complied with authority even when it meant potentially harming a patient.

This extreme example reveals something unsettling about human nature: our instinct to comply can override our judgment, ethical standards, and common sense. This is true not only in life-or-death situations but also in the decisions that shape the direction of our lives.

I was reminded of this a few years ago when my wife and I spent an afternoon with a couple who, like us, had recently become parents. When the topic of education came up, the father, a bank executive, said they planned to send their child to preschool as soon as possible to prepare her for "the routine of school and work to follow."

His reasoning reflected a common expectation: structured education leading to a conventional career. Did he see this as the best path or simply inevitable? I didn't ask. Either way, it's the norm. And there's nothing wrong with following this typical route, unless it's not the best one for you.

Early on, we learn that good kids "do as they're told." When a parent tells us to share our toys, or a teacher insists we raise our hand before speaking, we learn that following directions brings rewards, while defiance brings consequences. This early conformity enables learning and belonging. These needs don't expire after childhood. Throughout our lives, we want to be right, and we want to be liked.

But this tendency comes at a cost. We adopt false beliefs because everyone around us believes them. We follow paths we don't desire because social pressure makes alternatives seem impossible. We silence our doubts because speaking up feels dangerous.

The danger of social influence is that we fall into the trap of compliance by *letting others' opinions and expectations shape our choices, even when they clash with our personal truth or objective reality.*

As we grow up, social influence expands: friends, schools, workplaces, and online communities become our new tribes with their own rules. Ideally, we also develop the courage to challenge those that are false or harmful. In reality, we keep doing what we're told when we should think for ourselves.

TWO WAYS WE COMPLY

Social influence isn't a single force. It's a spectrum of pressures that range from subtle cues to explicit orders, from gentle nudges to forceful demands.

Consider two examples from the workplace:

You start arriving for work an hour early because your colleagues do. You've noticed you're less productive because of the longer hours and reduced sleep, yet you continue to show up early because everyone around you does.

Later that day, your manager asks you to prepare a strategy presentation. Although you disagree with the strategy's direction, you reluctantly obey.

In both situations, you're following social influence, but there's a crucial difference in how that influence gained your compliance. Your colleagues never requested you show up earlier; you were influenced simply by observing their behavior. With your manager, however, there was an explicit request that you obeyed.

This distinction between unintentional and intentional social influence helps explain why the compliance trap is so difficult to escape. We often recognize when we're being directly ordered to do something, but we're far less aware of how our social environment silently shapes our choices.

INVISIBLE PRESSURE

Social influence shapes our beliefs and behaviors even when no one demands we comply. We imitate others in everything from fashion and music to our beliefs and workplace habits.

Much of this is harmless. There's no real consequence to pretending to like your friends' music. Some influence is even positive, like exercising more because your friends do.

But we also mimic false beliefs and unproductive behaviors. Social influence even makes us ignore the evidence that's right in front of us—sometimes quite literally.

DOUBTING OUR OWN EYES

One famous example comes from Solomon Asch's 1950s experiments. Participants had to match a line's length to one of three options. The task was simple, and one choice was clearly correct. But the real test came when the group, made up of actors working with the researchers, deliberately chose the wrong answer. Under normal conditions, the error rate was below 1 percent. When faced with unanimous incorrect responses, 70 percent of participants conformed at least once, and the average error rate jumped to 37 percent.[51]

What makes these findings so telling is that people comply with social influence even when they know better. No one forced participants to choose the wrong answer. They simply followed the group. In the decades since this first experiment, results from over one hundred studies in seventeen countries have confirmed these findings.

I remember experiencing this firsthand as an eight-year-old. Our class assignment was to research the origin of the amusing Afrikaans saying, which translates to "it's so hot the crows are yawning." The answer, I discovered, was that yawning was a way for crows to cool down on hot days. But when my classmates all gave a different response, I doubted myself and repeated what they said. When I later realized I was right all along, I remember feeling upset and confused at my lack of self-confidence and willingness to conform to the group (even if I didn't have the vocabulary to express it that way yet).

That certainly wasn't the last time I fell into this trap. There have since been too many times I followed the consensus when I should have spoken up against it. Compliance is the default unless we deliberately resist. And resistance becomes even harder as the questions get more complex.

WHEN TRUTH GETS COMPLICATED

Some questions require effort and expertise to answer:

- Do humans cause climate change?
- Do vaccines cause autism?
- Do carbs make you fat?

These questions are important; a correct answer helps us avoid everything from an expanding waistline to an uninhabitable planet. However, they require more than just a personal observation or a quick search of the evidence. Unfortunately, another finding from the Asch studies was that when judgments are more complex, we are more likely to conform.[52]

This helps explain why conformity fuels conspiracy theories and fake news. It's not easy to determine whether a secret group is plotting global domination or if something more mundane is happening. Take Pizzagate, for example.

During the 2016 US election, a false claim spread online that high-ranking politicians ran a child-trafficking ring from a DC pizzeria. Despite being debunked by law enforcement and fact-checkers, it led one believer to storm the restaurant with a rifle, all because people kept repeating the story within their circles.

While these examples involve factual questions that can eventually be proven or disproven, the influence runs even deeper in areas where no objective truth exists.

THE SCRIPTS WE FOLLOW

Other "truths" are personal and subjective:

- What kind of career should I pursue?
- Is marriage necessary for a fulfilling life?
- What does success look like for me?

These answers involve preferences and values, not just objective facts. Yet social influence extends to these too. We absorb shared beliefs about how we should live, default norms shaped by our families and societies.

From childhood, we're conditioned to accept certain ideas as normal. Traditional gender roles paint men as breadwinners and women as caregivers. Formal education, university degrees, and specific career paths (doctor, lawyer, business owner) are seen as prestigious. Milestones like marriage, parenthood, and homeownership define adulthood. Even our view of relationships is shaped by societal norms, with monogamous nuclear families positioned as the standard. There are social templates for every major life decision.

Pew Research Center found that among Americans living with a partner, about a quarter said they felt "some" or "a lot" of pressure to marry that partner. Three-quarters said they felt pressure to be financially successful, and about four in ten women (and 27 percent of men) said they felt pressure to have children, regardless of their personal desires. Among US adults age fifty and older who have never had children, about 42 percent of women and 27 percent of men report that they felt pressure from society to have children when they were younger.[53]

These influences create a picture of what is typical, acceptable, and respectable. Most people rarely question these norms because they absorb them passively. But the source of this influence evolves throughout our lives.

CIRCLES OF INFLUENCE

As we grow, family influence is supplemented and sometimes replaced by peer influence. Friends, colleagues, and social circles shape new norms, often overriding our childhood conditioning. The pressure to fit in affects everything from the language we use to our career choices and parenting styles.

At first glance, adopting new peer norms may seem like nonconformity. But it's often just compliance in a different form. Fitting into a new social group requires following its rules, whether in fashion, politics, or ethics.

One study found that participants' opinions on political issues shifted an average of 30 percent toward their group's position after just fifteen minutes of discussion. More striking still: they left believing they had always held these revised views.

Beyond close relationships, we're also influenced by distant social influences from role models and social media.

Celebrities, entrepreneurs, and influencers shape our perceptions of success and desirability. We take their advice even in areas where they have no expertise. These public figures set artificial standards that impact our aspirations and lifestyle choices.

The average American now spends more time on digital media than with family, friends, or colleagues. Each hour shapes our perceptions of what's normal, desirable, and possible. Trends, memes, and online culture announce what's relevant, cool, or acceptable. Conforming to these digital norms provides a sense of belonging, even when the connection is artificial.

But perhaps most deceptive is when this conformity disguises itself as rebellion.

DIFFERENT UNIFORMS, SAME CONFORMITY

Of course, these influences can be empowering when they challenge outdated ideas, but they also spread superficial or commercialized visions of what's desirable. The counterculture movement that traps millions in mindless obedience isn't any different from the mainstream culture it opposes. It just replaces one set of norms with another.

As social critic Thomas Frank observed, "Rebellion is big business."[54] We mistake new conformity for true independence. The punk movement, which began as an anti-capitalist protest, became a fashion category at mall stores. Mindfulness meditation, once about nonattachment and inner peace, now sells corporate retreats and smartphone apps.

While rejecting tradition can be liberating, adopting countercultural ideals without question is just another form of conformity. Whether it's tradition or rebellion, both can become scripts we follow without critical thought. True independence comes not from reacting against the norm but from deciding what aligns with our values and sound reasoning.

What makes unintentional social influence so remarkable is that the pressure to comply comes almost entirely from within. Of course, that's not always the case. Sometimes, social influence exists in a gray area, like when influencers subtly shape our preferences, or when family expectations are communicated through both unspoken norms and direct conversations. The line between unintentional and intentional influence often blurs in real life. But in its most direct form, social influence is aimed at us as a subtle request or an explicit command.

DIRECT PRESSURE

"Because I said so." You've heard it before. From a parent when you were young or from a boss who didn't want to explain themselves. This isn't the indirect influence we've just explored, but rather it's a direct attempt to shape what you do or believe.

Not all intentional influence is harmful, of course. Parents steer children away from danger. Friends and mentors guide us through difficult decisions. Public health campaigns encourage us to wear seatbelts and quit smoking. These examples of deliberate influence often serve us well.

But there's another side. Even well-intentioned parents following their own biases might push children toward careers that fulfill the parents' dreams rather than the child's. Religious leaders might pressure followers to adopt beliefs that contradict evidence or common sense. Politicians and advertisers craft messages designed to make us act against our own interests while believing we're making free choices.

This is the realm of intentional social influence: the direct attempts to shape our behavior through requests, commands, appeals to authority, and cleverly designed "nudges." It's where compliance becomes less about mimicry and more about submission, and it happens all around us, every day.

OBEDIENCE

Parental influence works because we're naturally obedient to authority.

From our earliest moments, we learn that bigger, more powerful people make the rules. Parents tell children when to sleep and what to eat. Teachers instruct students. Bosses direct employees. This pattern extends everywhere: religious leaders guide followers, governments direct citizens, and in many relationships, one party holds more power than the other.

Some obedience is necessary; imagine soldiers debating each tactical decision during active combat. But when we stop questioning whether instructions make sense, it can lead to harm. Several famous experiments have shown just how far this obedience can go.

In the 1960s, Stanley Milgram's experiments at Yale revealed that 65 percent of ordinary people would administer what they believed were dangerous electric shocks to a stranger just because an authority figure calmly instructed them to continue.[55] The participants weren't sadists—they were suspending their personal responsibility when following orders.

Philip Zimbardo's Stanford Prison Experiment showed the same pattern. Student volunteers randomly assigned as "guards" or "prisoners" in a simulation quickly adopted these roles. The "guards" became increasingly cruel while the "prisoners" became passive. The experiment had to end early because the authority structure overwhelmed individual morality.[56]

The Hofling hospital experiment, which we opened this chapter with, demonstrated this same principle in a real-world setting, showing that professional training and ethical standards are easily overridden by the voice of authority.[57]

These experiments reveal our tendency to comply with authority, even when it violates our ethics or professional standards. This pattern plays out in countless less dramatic ways daily: accepting assignments that don't make sense because the boss requested them or deferring to experts despite contradictory evidence. Each small act of unquestioned obedience keeps us trapped in compliance.

But authority figures aren't the only source of this trap. What happens when authority becomes codified into formal rules and laws that govern entire societies? The pressure to conform becomes even more powerful, and the consequences for defiance become more severe.

WHEN COMPLIANCE IS LAW

Laws, rules, and policies are formalized versions of conformity, backed by legal penalties. Breaking the law carries a greater sense of wrongdoing than breaking a social norm like singing in a library.

But why?

We inherit laws we had no role in choosing. People created some laws centuries ago, but we follow them as unquestioned truths. Since laws vary widely across countries and even within countries, does that suggest some laws are better than others? The diversity in worldwide laws about abortion, drug use, and free speech demonstrate this clearly.

The reason for some laws is often circular. A striking example comes from the 2015 US Supreme Court case legalizing same-sex marriage. Chief Justice Roberts dissented, arguing that marriage had been heterosexual "for millennia," across cultures: "The Court invalidates the marriage laws of more than half the States and orders the transformation of a social institution that has formed the basis of human society for millennia, for the Kalahari Bushmen and the Han Chinese, the Carthaginians and the Aztecs. Just who do we think we are?"[58]

While Chief Justice Roberts's opinion did not sway the result, remarkably, the best reason why we have specific laws may be because they are what's always been done.

This isn't an argument for lawlessness, but laws should be scrutinized like any other social norm.

Many laws that once seemed sensible—prohibitions against

interracial marriage or women voting—now appear as obvious injustices. The most profound progress begins when we question laws that everyone has long taken for granted.

Not all intentional influence is as direct as a law or command, however. Some of the most effective forms of influence are designed to be nearly invisible, guiding our choices while preserving the illusion of freedom.

NUDGING

Have you ever wondered why you ended up with that streaming service you barely use? Or why are you paying for the "premium" version of an app when the basic one would do? Chances are you were nudged.

Nudging is an influence designed to preserve the illusion of choice while subtly directing you toward a particular option. Behavioral economists Richard Thaler and Cass Sunstein popularized this concept in their 2009 book *Nudge*. One key insight from the book is that setting something as the default option dramatically increases the chances people will choose it.[59]

Sometimes nudges genuinely help us. Automatic enrollment in retirement plans increases savings rates by 75 percent.[60] Opt-out organ donation policies in countries like Spain result in donation rates above 90 percent, compared to around 15 percent in opt-in countries like the United States.[61] These defaults simplify our lives by making the beneficial choice the path of least resistance.

But for every helpful nudge, there are dozens designed purely to extract value from us. A McDonald's delivery app (researched purely for science, of course) shows this in action: the default meal includes medium fries and soda. To remove them or select a smaller portion requires extra effort, something most people avoid.

These "dark nudges" are manipulative defaults that benefit the designer of the choice, not the one making the choice:

- Free trials that silently convert to paid subscriptions
- Pre-checked boxes for marketing emails
- Fast-food apps that default to larger, more expensive portions

Recognizing the potential for misuse, Thaler later warned about the "Power of Nudges for Good and Bad" in the *New York Times*.[62] He recounted a dark nudge he experienced when attempting to read a review of his latest book published by the *Times of London*. To read the article, he would have to subscribe, but he was reluctant since there was an automatic renewal clause and an onerous cancellation process.

He criticized dark nudges that violate three ethical principles: lack of transparency, difficulty in opting out, and lack of benefit to the consumer over the corporation.

Ironically, while reading Thaler's piece on unethical nudges, I clicked a link for the *New York Times*'s subscription offer. The fine print revealed an automatic renewal and a complex cancellation process, exactly the kind of misleading nudge he warned against.

The key difference between helpful and harmful nudges isn't the technique but the intent and transparency. Ethical nudges are transparent about what they're doing, make opting out easy, and genuinely benefit the person being nudged, not just the nudger.

When faced with intentional influence, whether a direct command or a subtle nudge, the essential question isn't "Should I comply?" but "Who benefits most from my compliance?" The answer reveals whether you're being guided or manipulated.

DON'T TRUST STRANGERS

"Don't trust strangers" is advice we've all heard since childhood. It's time we applied it later in life too.

Every act of compliance is really an act of trusting strangers. Whether they are strangers on the internet, companies with their own interests, or gurus and role models. We follow trends because strangers say they're worth following. We adopt beliefs because strangers tell us they're true. We pursue careers because strangers assure us they're valuable.

What's harder to appreciate is that even our close relations are strangers to our internal desires and goals. Your family, friends, and colleagues can never fully know your innermost thoughts and motivations. In some ways, we are all strangers to each other's subjective experiences. The people closest to us may understand us better than total strangers, and they might truly have our best interests in mind. But they can never fully know our private inner world.

Yes, connection and community are important. The trouble begins when we surrender our judgment to others, and when we let their opinions override our inner voice because they speak with authority or conviction.

This applies equally to our subjective experience and to objective reality. Just as others can't determine who you truly are, no amount of agreement can change reality. As Bertrand Russell put it, "The fact that an opinion has been widely held is no evidence whatever that it is not utterly absurd; indeed, in view of the silliness of the majority of mankind, a widespread belief is more likely to be foolish than sensible."[63] Groups can be just as wrong about objective truths as they can be clueless about your personal desires.

So listen to the well-meaning advice of those around you and admire your role models. But see it for what it is: guidance from a stranger, not the last word.

The compliance trap closes when we realize that no consensus, no matter how widespread, can change objective reality or overrule the facts. And no one else, no matter how close, credible, or confident, can tell you who you are. Trust yourself.

CHAPTER FOUR

The Complacency Trap

DO YOU REMEMBER A TIME WHEN "GOING TO WORK" meant leaving the house?

When the pandemic forced everyone to work from home, we discovered that most desk jobs could be done just as well, or even better, remotely. Going to the office turned out to be less about necessity and more about the way things had always been done.

This pattern of accepting long-standing practices without question appears everywhere. Consider a popular story about NASA's Space Shuttle solid rocket boosters (SRBs). According to the tale, these massive engineering marvels were exactly 4 feet 8.5 inches wide, a measurement supposedly dictated by ancient Roman chariots. The story traces a chain of inheritance: the SRBs had to fit on railway cars for transport; American railways adopted British standards, which evolved from tramways, which followed ruts in old Roman roads, which were sized for two horses pulling a chariot.

So one of humanity's most advanced technological achievements was constrained by a measurement determined thousands of years earlier by the width of two horses' rear ends.

It's a remarkable story that perfectly illustrates how arbitrary decisions echo through time. Remarkable, but false. Many parts of the story are incorrect or oversimplified. Yet it spread widely because it feels true. We recognize this pattern of unquestioned inheritance everywhere.

The QWERTY keyboard layout, designed to prevent typewriter keys from jamming, persists on our touchscreen devices. Early cars were called "horseless carriages" and maintained familiar carriage shapes despite completely different mechanical needs. When newspapers went digital, they simply copied their print layouts to screens instead of exploring the new medium's possibilities.

This reveals something fundamental about how we think. The world is full of "rules" that aren't really rules at all. They're just the way things have always been done. These assumptions become so normalized that we stop questioning them. Every environment we encounter comes preloaded with traditions and practices we accept without examination.

It's true that some things have "stood the test of time." There can be wisdom in ideas, institutions, and practices that have endured. The entire basis for learning is observing what's worked in the past.

But "we've always done it this way" isn't sufficient justification by itself. History shows us that many long-held beliefs and customs were eventually proved to be wrong or harmful when people examined them carefully. What worked in the past might not be optimal today, especially as circumstances change. We should also consider who benefits from maintaining the status quo. Often, "tradition" is defended most vigorously by those who profit from it.

The tendency to assume that because things *are* a certain way, they *should* be that way is what philosophers call the

Is-Ought Fallacy, first articulated by David Hume.[64] A variation is the naturalistic fallacy: the belief that what's "natural" is inherently good and what's "artificial" is suspect. It's an idea that quickly collapses when we consider deadly natural poisons and life-saving artificial medicines. "Natural" and "traditional" aren't synonyms for "good" and "right."

Yet these fallacies are embedded in our psychology as biases that lead us to prefer the familiar and long-standing over the new and different. They trap us in complacency: *accepting the world as it is without question, missing opportunities for positive change.*

Complacency doesn't depend on past behaviors or others' influence. It's the tendency to accept our environment without examination, and it's the third and perhaps most pervasive trap of conformity.

THE WAY IT IS

This chapter explores three powerful psychological forces that make us complacent about the status quo.

First, we'll examine existence and longevity bias, our tendency to prefer things simply because they exist or have existed for a long time. From New Coke's spectacular failure to our skepticism of new technologies, we'll see how the mere age of something can make us view it more favorably, regardless of its actual merit.

Next, we'll look at how we become trapped by inherited choices, which are decisions made by others that we accept without question. Whether it's doctors inheriting another physician's diagnosis or organizations maintaining outdated systems, we often stick with previous decisions even when circumstances have changed and better options are available.

Finally, we'll explore system justification, our surprising tendency to defend existing systems, even when they harm us. This powerful bias leads disadvantaged groups to support structures that work against their interests and makes us resistant to beneficial changes that could improve our lives.

IF IT EXISTS, IT'S GOOD

In his famous song, John Lennon asked us to imagine a different and better world. It's not hard to imagine all the ways the world could be better than it is today. Yet we often fall into a subtle trap: preferring things just because they exist.

Research reveals this bias in action. Scott Eidelman and colleagues conducted an experiment where participants were shown a picture of what appeared to be a galaxy but was actually just a collection of random data points. The participants were divided into three groups and told that either 40, 60, or 80 percent of galaxies looked like this. The more common participants thought these constellations were, the more beautiful they perceived them to be.[65] This study reveals an *existence bias*, where the mere existence of something leads us to view it more favorably.

In further work, Eidelman, and his collaborators found evidence of a related bias, where longer existence is judged to be better. In one example of this *longevity bias*, participants were given a description of acupuncture and told that it was anywhere from five hundred to two thousand years old. Consistent with their hypothesis, the longer it was said to exist, the more people thought it was effective, and the more likely they were to promote its use.[66]

This same effect was found in many other contexts. People preferred the same picture of a tree when told it was older, and they preferred the taste of chocolate more when it was said to have been on the market for longer.

The Coca-Cola Company learned about this bias firsthand when it launched "New Coke" in the 1980s.

For several years before that point, Coca-Cola's market share was falling, while Pepsi's was on the rise. Blind taste tests showed that consumers preferred Pepsi, but Coke was still holding strong. However, the company was worried about losing market share. Coca-Cola spent over two years and millions to develop a new formula that outperformed Pepsi in blind taste tests. However, when New Coke was introduced, the public was not impressed. They received over forty thousand letters and four hundred thousand phone calls from angry customers and brought back the old formula, while New Coke was gradually pulled off the market.

Coke seemed to get a lot right in its innovation process. They conducted over nineteen thousand blind taste tests and launched an ad campaign with Bill Cosby (still an appealing character at the time) pushing the message that "New Is Good."[67] But they ignored the powerful bias for familiarity the brand had relied on.

The story of New Coke contains evidence of people's longevity bias. The longer something has existed, the better we perceive it to be. Coke had established a long history by the 1980s, and this change to the formula tainted the heritage of the brand and product.

This same bias affects us in many important ways too.

As new technologies are introduced, we become resistant to change, even when innovations are helpful. In one study, people were given different technologies to review and were told that some were invented before their birth and others after. Again, the finding showed this same bias: older technologies were viewed more favorably and new ones more skeptically.[68] Instead of evaluating the benefits and risks objectively, we rely on tradition to shape our preferences.

Perhaps the most significant illustration of this bias is found in a study that shows how even contentious practices can gain support when characterized as long-standing. A group of US adults were randomly assigned to read about the use of "enhanced interrogations" in the "War on Terror" by the US government. They were told it was either a new tactic or a practice that has been used for over forty years. When torture was described as a long-standing practice, it received more support and was seen as more effective and justifiable than when it was described as new.[69]

Existence and longevity biases shape many aspects of modern life. Consider how many practices we follow simply because "we've always done it that way"—the forty-hour workweek, conventional schooling, retirement age, voting systems, and criminal justice approaches. The recent shift to remote work during the pandemic revealed how one such tradition, office-based work, persisted mainly through custom rather than necessity.

The fact that some of these have started to change only proves the point: for a long time, we followed tradition without good reason.

The workplace is responsible for many examples of this bias. People execute procedures without regard for why they are doing the thing in the first place. In some companies, "we've always done it that way" or simply "that's how it's done" is the unofficial mantra.

In all these cases, the only sensible response is "Why?"

But our tendency to accept the world as it is runs deeper than just preferring what exists. We also blindly accept choices that were made for us long ago.

INHERITED CHOICES

When you started your current job, you likely inherited processes and tools designed by your predecessors. You didn't choose these systems. They were chosen for you. Yet you continue to use them all the same.

This pattern extends far beyond the workplace. One common way we become complacent about our status quo is when we inherit others' choices. Unlike direct social pressure or our own habits, these decisions were made in the past by different people in different circumstances. Yet we accept them as our own, continuing down paths chosen by others because they've been chosen before.

I've discussed one example of this before. In Samuelson and Zeckhauser's famous 1988 paper, which introduced the term "Status Quo bias," one experiment asked people to imagine they had inherited funds from a deceased great-uncle. When one group was told the funds were already invested in a portfolio by their uncle, they showed a larger tendency to retain the investment than those deciding without a status quo.[70]

This pattern of defaulting to inherited choices affects everything from high-stakes medical decisions to organizational strategies, creating a hidden but powerful form of complacency.

Physicians are often called to provide a second opinion after a prior decision by another expert. A 2021 study from Australia tested how physicians handle these inherited decisions. Participants were asked to choose between two equally effective treatments for a patient, with three test conditions: no previous recommendation, a previous recommendation for treatment A, or a previous recommendation for treatment B.[71]

The results were striking. Without a prior recommendation, 39 percent chose treatment A, and 61 percent chose B. However, when treatment A was presented as the previous doctor's choice,

74 percent selected it. When B was the inherited choice, 85 percent went with it. Physicians were significantly more influenced by these inherited choices than the general public in the study.[72] These experts, whom we rely on to be objective with our health at stake, changed their medical recommendations just because another physician had made a prior assessment.

The workplace is a prime example of the real-life impact of this. Those stepping into a new role often inherit many legacy decisions that may need to be reevaluated. The software system that no longer meets the needs of the business but is familiar and doesn't involve the time and cost involved with switching. The hierarchical organization structure that strains collaboration but is what people have come to know. The ten-year strategy the new CEO is saddled with fulfilling five years down the line that is starting to look out of touch with reality. In each scenario, a strong case can be made for change, but since we've inherited this status quo, we stick with it, for better or worse.

In many of these cases, we seem to prefer the risk of "failing conventionally," as described by Annie Duke in *Quit*:

> John Maynard Keynes, one of the most influential economists of the twentieth century, summed up this phenomenon well when he said, "Worldly wisdom teaches that it is better for reputation to fail conventionally than to succeed unconventionally." Succeeding unconventionally carries with it the risk of experiencing failure as a result of veering from the status quo.
>
> A higher chance of failing is more tolerated on paths that don't rock the boat. After all, what's the go-to defense in a postmortem after we make a decision that doesn't work out? "I followed procedure," or "I stuck with the status quo," or "I made the consensus choice."

Failing conventionally doesn't feel as bad, nor is it treated as such by the people who are judging you.[73]

Of course, failing conventionally is still failing. And we could all do better by risking improvement instead of hiding behind the comfort of convention.

Yet complacency manifests in an even more paradoxical way. Not only do we accept things as they are, but we also actively defend systems that don't serve us well or might even harm us. This puzzling phenomenon, known as system justification, reveals one of the most perplexing dimensions of our relationship with the status quo.

JUSTIFYING INJUSTICE

In 1980, psychologist Melvin Lerner documented a troubling tendency: people often blame victims for their own misfortunes. This "just world" belief helps people maintain the comforting illusion that the world is fair and orderly, and people get what they deserve.[74]

This laid the groundwork for what John Jost and Mahzarin Banaji would later formalize as the *system justification theory*. Their work revealed something even more surprising: people don't just rationalize individual misfortunes; they defend entire social systems, even when those systems work against their interests.[75]

The evidence is striking. Studies find that both men and women show bias favoring men in leadership roles. And research also shows a "pro-white" leadership bias: minority and majority participants alike are more likely to associate white individuals with leadership traits and to evaluate white candidates more favorably in hypothetical organizational contexts.[76]

A 2004 meta-analysis of a decade of research confirmed this pattern across multiple cultures and social systems.[77] Disadvantaged groups—including ethnic minorities, poor people, and LGBTQ+ individuals—frequently endorsed views that legitimized their own lower status.

System justification affects everyone, privileged and disadvantaged alike. It's a cognitive tendency that helps us make sense of our world by assuming the existing arrangements must serve some purpose, even when they don't.

The implications of system justification are profound, influencing how we perceive and interact with the world. It makes us accept and rationalize norms, ideas, practices, and institutions that are discriminatory or oppressive. It makes us accept things as "the way they are" when we should challenge them to improve the status quo.

This tendency affects many areas of life. In workplaces, employees often accept unfair practices like unequal pay or excessive workloads as "just the way things are." They may view hierarchical power structures as natural and resist changes that could benefit them. Leaders are seen as inherently more deserving of their positions, which reinforces the status quo.

Ironically, when unfair practices exist, system justification also makes us resistant to beneficial changes that could improve these systems. Employees might view these changes as unnecessary or harmful, preferring the familiar status quo even when improvements could benefit the organization and themselves.

Beyond work, people justify restrictive gender roles, inefficient bureaucracies, and outdated systems by assuming they serve necessary functions. This resistance to change persists even when better alternatives exist.

Most remarkably, system justification affects those who suffer most under unfair systems. The people with the greatest incentive to change things often become their most steadfast defenders. This isn't because they lack awareness or intelligence but because accepting the fundamental unfairness of a system we're embedded in is psychologically threatening. It's easier to believe the world is fair than to acknowledge we're trapped in structures designed without our interests in mind.

This reveals the strongest evidence of complacency: We don't just passively accept the status quo. We actively work to maintain it, even against our self-interest. We become guardians of gates that keep us locked outside. By defending these systems, we give them the legitimacy they haven't earned and the power they don't deserve.

THE GIVEN AND THE GRADUAL

Throughout this chapter, we've examined how complacency, our uncritical acceptance of the world as it is, shapes our lives. I've focused on how we accept long-standing environmental defaults: preferring what exists simply because it exists, accepting inherited choices without question, and defending systems that may not serve us well.

But complacency has another, equally powerful dimension. We not only accept static elements of our environment unquestioningly, but we also fail to notice gradual shifts that change our world little by little. Milton Mayer, reflecting on the experiences of ordinary Germans during the rise of Nazi Germany, vividly captured this second form of complacency in his book *They Thought They Were Free*:

> Step C is not so much worse than Step B, and, if you did not make a stand at Step B, why should you at Step C? And so on to Step D.[78]

Step by step, each tiny compromise makes the next one easier. We adjust our standards of what's acceptable until we accept circumstances we would have outright rejected if presented with them all at once. Eventually, Mayer describes a profound psychological moment of clarity:

> Suddenly it all comes down, all at once. You see what you are, what you have done, or, more accurately, what you haven't done (for that was all that was required of most of us: that we do nothing).[79]

This story is intense and disturbing, set against one of the most significant human tragedies in history. Thankfully, most of us will never confront such extremes. However, Mayer's account reveals something universal about how complacency operates: whether we accept long-standing defaults or gradually shift standards, we drift into circumstances we'd never consciously choose.

Bertrand Russell once observed that "the world is a higgledy-piggledy place, containing things pleasant and things unpleasant in haphazard sequence."[80] Our complacency makes us accept this world simply because it *is*. We mistake what exists for what should be and what has been for what must be.

Yet progress, both individually and collectively, depends on seeing the current state of the world as just one possibility among many. The status quo isn't inevitable. It's contingent, shaped by countless decisions and circumstances that could have been different. And if it could have been different, it still can be.

Part II

The Defiant Mindset

NOW YOU SEE THE TRAPS. YOU KNOW HOW CONFORMITY has been running your life. Your first instinct might be to rebel against everything, but mindless rebellion is just another trap. What you need is a new way of thinking. The chapters ahead teach you to develop this mindset. You'll learn what Rational Defiance actually means, how to see clearly without filters, where to find ideas that expand what's possible, and why experimenting beats endless planning. This isn't about becoming a contrarian who rejects everything. It's about knowing when to conform and when to defy—and having the tools to tell the difference. That's where we go next.

CHAPTER FIVE

Rational Defiance

IN THE EARLY 1990S, JERRY STERNIN LED THE SAVE THE Children program, which aimed to reduce malnutrition in Vietnamese villages. His team had minimal funding and little institutional backing. What they had was the willingness to look where others hadn't.

With limited resources, the team discovered local families who nourished their children despite the widespread starvation. These families did things differently: feeding their children even when they were sick, offering smaller meals throughout the day, incorporating nutrient-rich foods others discarded, and actively feeding their children instead of simply placing food in front of them. These practices were unconventional and effective.[81]

Sternin's team promoted the practices of these families in these communities. Within two years, malnutrition was reduced by 65 to 85 percent across the villages.[82] This case led to the development of the positive deviance movement, which amplifies effective unconventional practices in communities globally. It has since impacted the lives of thirty million people in sixty countries.[83]

* * *

Born in postwar Austria in 1947, Arnold Schwarzenegger grew up feeling like he didn't belong. In the 2023 Netflix documentary about his life, he recalls:

> When I was in school already, I felt like I didn't belong here. I belonged somewhere else. That's not the life I want to live, like the Austrians live their life, which is, you know, go to school until eighteen, get married, have kids. Just work to support your family. I thought that my purpose in life was just far beyond that.[84]

So instead of conforming to his environment, he left to pursue bodybuilding, a niche sport at the time. Despite his modest background, he achieved unprecedented success. He won the Mr. Olympia title multiple times and became the most famous figure in the sport.

At the pinnacle of his fame as a bodybuilder, Schwarzenegger again felt he had outgrown that version of his life and pursued acting. People told him his accent, size, and name would never work in Hollywood; however, he became an iconic action star of the twentieth century.

Instead of being satisfied with being a seven-time Olympia winner and the most famous action star of his era, Arnold pivoted again. He entered politics and ran for Governor of California. As a political outsider with no prior experience, he faced significant doubts. Nonetheless, he won the election and served two terms, leaving behind a legacy that is uniquely his.

* * *

Dick Fosbury was an American high jumper who competed in the 1960s, but he couldn't master the sport's dominant technique: the straddle. It had been used for decades, where athletes went over the bar face-down, lifting a straight lead leg in the air.

As a teenager, the straddle technique cost Fosbury repeated missed attempts and head-on crashes into the bar. He later recalled, "I knew I had to change my body position, and that's what started first the revolution, and over the next two years, the evolution."[85]

He experimented by curling up on his back and lifting his body sideways to clear the bar. That's how the unconventional "Fosbury Flop" was born.

When Fosbury first used the technique in competition in 1963, it was ridiculed by coaches and fellow competitors. A newspaper even labeled him the "World's Laziest High Jumper."[86] However, Fosbury persisted.

His unorthodox style paid off at the 1968 Mexico City Olympics, where Fosbury won the gold medal and set an Olympic record at 2.24 meters using his back-first flop.

Within a few years, the Fosbury Flop became the dominant technique in the global high-jump community. Fosbury's courage to challenge the status quo fundamentally changed his sport. Today, he is recognized as one of the most influential athletes of the last century.

* * *

These stories come from different places: public health, personal ambition, and athletic innovation. But they share a deeper similarity: each began with someone confronting the pull of conformity and choosing to defy it. But they didn't rebel blindly. They pursued something better and with purpose.

They practiced what I call Rational Defiance: *the deliberate decision to challenge the status quo when it stands in the way of something better.*

Rational Defiance might sound like a contradiction. We think of defiance as emotional, impulsive, even reckless. But the most effective nonconformists don't break rules for the thrill of it. They break them because they see a better way. This type of nonconformity is grounded in four key principles:

- **Better** in pursuit of meaningful improvement
- **Selective** in choosing what's worth resisting
- **Deliberate** by acting out of awareness, not instinct
- **Different** enough to break from convention

Of these, the easiest to recognize is defiance: a refusal to conform and a willingness to take unconventional actions. Yet not all defiance is wise. But when driven by the desire to make things better—and applied selectively and deliberately—it can transform lives, systems, and even entire fields.

This chapter is about this kind of thoughtful defiance. In the pages ahead, we'll explore its principles and transform your understanding of defiance from a risky rebellion into a rational strategy for meaningful change.

BETTER: IMPROVEMENT IS THE GOAL

The goal of Rational Defiance isn't to rebel but to improve. When today's reality stands in the way, they challenge it. Whether it's keeping children fed and healthy, chasing a personal vision, or excelling in their field, the people in the earlier stories defied the norm to reach something better. Often, that improvement is measurable.

Fosbury's new technique let him jump higher than the old one. Sternin's work in Vietnam led to healthier children. In both cases, the results were clear: the new approach worked better than what came before.

This happens in everyday life too. A team leader finds a better way to work. A teacher reshapes their classroom and sees engagement rise. Someone changes their habits and sees improvements in energy, weight, or health.

Even beliefs can be tested this way. Scientific breakthroughs often begin with defiance. For centuries, people believed disease came from bad air. Then germ theory arrived with evidence. It challenged a long-standing idea and proved there's a better way to understand disease.

When outcomes are measurable, the case for defiance is obvious. The numbers speak for themselves: higher, healthier, more efficient. But limiting ourselves to measurable outcomes would miss half the story. Not every version of "better" shows up in numbers. Some of the most important improvements in life can only be felt, not counted.

Take Arnold Schwarzenegger. He didn't just defy other people's expectations; he reinvented himself constantly. There was no proof that leaving Austria for bodybuilding was the right move. It was just a belief that he was meant for something more.

His life afterward followed that same pattern. People said he'd never make it in Hollywood. Then they said he'd never make it in politics. At every step, he chose what felt right for him. The payoff wasn't measured in metrics but in a life that matched the vision he had for himself. As he explained, "If you don't have a vision of where you're going and if you don't have a goal where you go, you drift around, and you never end up anywhere...You will not end up anywhere or most likely in the wrong place."[87] The alignment between inner vision and outer life is its own form of success.

The same principle applies to anyone who refuses to accept a life that feels misaligned with their values. Whether you're leaving a safe job to pursue your passion, rejecting cultural norms to live more authentically, or opting for a different kind of family structure, if it feels more aligned and honest, it counts. Defiance is rational when it leads to a better version of reality, even if the only person who can see it is you.

Here's the caveat: once you start seeing opportunities for improvement, you'll spot them everywhere. Every system seems broken. Every tradition feels outdated. Every norm appears arbitrary. But seeking improvement everywhere is not the aim. That way lies exhaustion and ineffectiveness. It's deciding which areas are worth improving in the first place.

SELECTIVE: CHOOSE YOUR BATTLES

Rational Defiance is about knowing what's worth fighting for. Some things are better left unchanged. Not because they're perfect but because they're not the problem worth defying. Rational Defiance is selective.

The Conformity Coma is a constant state of status quo acceptance. But Rational Defiance is not a constant state of rebellion against the norm. There are countless things that can be improved. But living in a constant state of rebellion is exhausting and unproductive. Every class has a disruptive student, every workplace a troublemaker, and every social group a contrarian. In most of these cases, defiance is the only aim, and disruption is the only outcome.

True rational deviants understand something these constant rebels don't: most battles aren't worth fighting. Power comes from choosing the few that are.

That's why rational deviants are strategic conformists. Defiance isn't a spectrum from cautious to bold, with the goal of being defiant most of the time. It's a strategy of infrequent but meaningful acts of defiance conducted within a foundation of stability that makes those acts possible and effective.

Nassim Taleb proposed an investment approach that is a useful analogy for this idea. He calls it the barbell strategy. He suggests placing the majority of your assets in extremely safe investments, such as government bonds, while allocating a small portion to highly speculative, high-upside bets. You avoid the fragile middle (where the risk is still high and reward isn't meaningful) and instead strike a balance between two extremes: maximum safety on one end and maximum upside on the other. The result is that you preserve your downside while staying open to transformative opportunities.

This same principle applies to Rational Defiance. It's a kind of psychological barbell strategy. Most of the time, you conform, not out of weakness but out of strategy. You follow the default when it's harmless, when it's efficient, when it's just not worth the fight. But you reserve your limited energy and attention for high-leverage defiance—bold bets against the status quo where the upside is too important to ignore.

As Adam Grant notes in *Originals*, the most successful innovators are often conservative in other areas of their lives: "If you're about to bet aggressively in blackjack, you might drive below the speed limit on your way to the casino."[88] Strategic conformity provides the stability and resources for meaningful defiance where it matters. The key is identifying opportunities for defiance that are both valuable and meaningful.

Valuable: Some problems matter more than others. Some are annoyances. But others touch on things that deeply matter to you: who you are, how you live, what you believe. A dress code might be annoying, but an unhappy career? That's valuable to challenge. And some are valuable because they matter deeply in the world around you—pressing problems that deserve to be challenged.

Meaningful: Some acts of defiance offer only marginal gains. Others change you or the world around you in a fundamental way. Switching from one productivity app to another might save you five minutes. Redesigning how your entire team works can transform an organization.

Rational Defiance lives at the intersection. Where the problem matters and where the payoff could be significant.

Saying no to a default script that doesn't fit who you are can alter the course of your life. Challenging an outdated norm can benefit everyone when the stakes are high and the payoff is meaningful.

Even the smallest acts pass this test, like redesigning your habits to reclaim time, health, or focus. The actions may seem minor, but they touch everything. And the change is meaningful because it compounds. Speaking up can be Rational Defiance. Not because it's loud but because it breaks a silence that keeps the status quo in place. When the issue matters and no one else will say it, one voice can change the room.

Rational Defiance doesn't mean constant resistance. It means choosing your battles and making them count. But there's a difference between those who stumble into the right fights by accident and those who choose them deliberately. This distinction matters more than it seems.

DELIBERATE: ACT WITH AWARENESS

Ted Williams and Ty Cobb stand among baseball's greatest hitters. Their statistics speak for themselves: Williams with his .344 lifetime batting average and Cobb with his even more remarkable .366. But beyond these numbers lies a fascinating contrast in how they approached their craft.

Williams was famous for his analytical approach to hitting. He meticulously studied the science of the swing, breaking down the strike zone into seventy-seven cells in his classic book, *The Science of Hitting*, and calculated his expected batting average for each cell.[89] Williams understood hitting so thoroughly that he could explain it to anyone, articulating precisely why certain mechanics worked and how to replicate his success.

Cobb, while equally effective at the plate, approached hitting more instinctively. He was known for his aggressive approach that seemed to come naturally to him. While Cobb certainly worked hard at his batting, he relied more on feel and competitive intensity than systematic analysis.

Life is full of examples of Williams versus Cobb's style of success. Some people succeed due to skill, luck, or circumstance, while others master principles that make success repeatable. For everyone who does well, only some understand *why* they do well.

This distinction between instinctively finding success and deliberately mastering it marks the next principle of Rational Defiance: deliberate intent.

From the outside, acts of successful defiance may look the same, but they're not. The people whose stories I share in this book weren't trying to be rational deviants. They didn't act with frameworks or philosophies in mind. For most, a combination of luck, circumstance, and inclination led them to act in this way. They broke from convention in an important area and achieved better results. They acted deliberately, but theirs is an in-the-moment intention to act differently to achieve something better. They recognized how their situation could be improved and took unconventional actions.

It's the kind of defiance you already know the power of. If you look hard enough, you can find your own examples of Rational Defiance, where you disobeyed convention and achieved something you're proud of. But most of us stumbled into these outcomes without knowing what we were doing and why. That's why few of us recognize this as a strategy that should be developed and applied more broadly.

The real power is recognizing the principle of Rational Defiance: when you understand that this approach is something you can apply repeatedly across different areas of life, it becomes a skill and a mindset, not just a onetime occurrence.

The difference is like someone who accidentally takes a scenic route versus someone who deliberately chooses to explore new paths. You end up in the same place, but the ability to discover new paths in the future is entirely different.

The stories in this book follow the clues about what it takes to be a strategic nonconformist. It's easy to feel at a disadvantage compared to someone with Arnold's determination or Fosbury's innovative spirit. Due to nature or nurture, some seem to find it easier to defy their status quo.

But just because they moved on instinct doesn't mean we have to. Rational Defiance isn't a talent reserved for the bold or brilliant. With deliberate intent, it's an approach that can be studied and applied repeatedly. It becomes a choice to act defiantly on purpose.

DIFFERENT: BE WILLING TO STAND APART

Different might seem like the most obvious principle of Rational Defiance. After all, if you're not doing something different, how can you be defying anything? But the subtlety is that being different isn't the goal, it's the outcome.

When the situation demands improvement, when the stakes are high, and when the choice is deliberate, it becomes clear that defiance is the answer. That's when it's rational to act differently from your past self, from others, or from the world around you.

Not all improvement requires defiance. You can improve without defying: mastering existing methods, refining established skills, and climbing traditional ladders.

Perfecting the traditional high-jump form is still progress; it just takes practice. The villagers in Vietnam could have followed the accepted nutrition advice more strictly. Arnold could have doubled down on bodybuilding or acting, rather than reinventing himself.

These are the routes of conventional mastery. They stay within the boundaries of what's already there. You get promoted within your field, master an existing genre, or build on an established scientific theory. But even if the results are impressive, they don't require breaking from the status quo.

But Rational Defiance asks for more. It leaves the existing path instead of improving it. The test is whether your action breaks cleanly enough from convention to stand apart. Not every improvement is defiant. But every act of Rational Defiance is unmistakably different.

Defiant acts meet four conditions:

Uniquely different: Rational Defiance isn't about being radically different by some universal standard; it's about breaking from *your* particular status quo. What counts as defiant depends on the expectations you've internalized, the norms you're surrounded by, and the path you're already on.

Schwarzenegger faced the pressure of consistency. He was already a global icon in the bodybuilding world. Switching to acting and then to politics defied the path he was on. The villagers in Vietnam faced the pressure of social consensus about feeding children. Instead of following it more strictly, they ran small experiments of their own. Fosbury faced the pressure of tradition. High jumping had been done one way for decades, and every coach, athlete, and commentator expected it to stay that way. His now-famous technique was a clear break from that tradition.

Defiance looks different for everyone. Becoming an artist in a family of lawyers is a defiant act. Becoming an artist in a family of artists may be conformity. What matters is the gap between what's expected of you and what you choose instead.

Radically divergent: Rational Defiance doesn't deviate slightly; it diverges from the path entirely. Incremental improvement asks, "How can we make this 10 percent better?" Rational Defiance asks, "What if we didn't do this at all?"

Better email gives us improved spam filters and faster servers. But Slack wasn't better email; it was an alternative approach to team communication. Fosbury didn't tweak the straddle technique; he abandoned it. The Vietnamese families didn't bend the nutrition guidelines. They invented their own.

This radical divergence separates defiance from mere improvement.

Invites resistance: Real defiance creates friction. The status quo resists change, especially when that change threatens established norms, authority, or comfort.

Coaches, reporters, and even fellow athletes mocked Fosbury for his unconventional jump. People dismissed Schwarzenegger as a bodybuilder who couldn't act, and then as an actor who couldn't govern. Galileo faced prison. Rosa Parks was arrested. Entrepreneurs are told they're crazy until they're proven right.

Even minor acts draw resistance. Push back against an unhealthy norm at work, and you might face subtle exclusion.

Express a belief that doesn't align with your social group, and you'll feel the tension. Question a long-standing tradition, and watch how quickly people defend "the way things have always been done."

If no one flinches, you might not have left the status quo at all. Resistance isn't the goal, but it's often the sign that you're doing something genuinely different.

Truly independent: Being different doesn't mean joining a different herd. It means thinking for yourself.

Too often, people escape one form of conformity only to fall into another. They leave corporate life to join a startup culture, trading one uniform for another. They reject mainstream values to adopt counterculture one's wholesale. They stop following their parents' expectations only to follow those of their peer group instead.

True Rational Defiance means being willing to stand alone if necessary. Not to be a contrarian but to be authentic. It means your choices come from your evaluation of what's better, not from any group's prescription of mainstream or alternative.

Sometimes this means your defiance might not even look defiant. In a social group of rebels, choosing stability might be the most independent path. In a culture that celebrates disruption, choosing to preserve something valuable might be an act of courage.

* * *

These four principles—Better, Selective, Deliberate, and Different—define Rational Defiance. Without improvement as the goal, you're just rebelling. Without selectivity, you're exhausting yourself. Without deliberation, you're relying on luck. And without being genuinely different, you're not defying anything.

When all four align, something powerful happens. You stop floating with the tide and swim with purpose.

DEFIANCE BIG AND SMALL

Most people conform reflexively, and some rebel impulsively. Rational Defiance offers a third way: thoughtful resistance where it counts. Once you understand these principles, you'll recognize them everywhere. People throughout history and across domains have practiced this philosophy, even though they didn't call it that.

In business, Roelof Botha of Sequoia Capital captured it: "If you're going to be really successful in this business, you have to be contrarian—and right."[90] He saw it when he invested early in YouTube and Instagram, decisions that initially seemed irrational but ultimately transformed entire industries.

> There's a little defiance in saying, "We'll show you!" I remember in 2001, when I was at PayPal, there was an article titled "Earth to Palo Alto." It said we were deranged, we didn't know what we were doing. In the meantime, I was inside the building, knowing that we were months away from being profitable and on our way to being a public company.[91]

And while his world is investing, the same pattern shows up everywhere.

In science, they call it a paradigm shift when someone challenges accepted theory and replaces it with something better. In art, it's creativity. In social movements, it's activism. Each field has its own name for the same underlying pattern: the deliberate choice to abandon the conventional path when you see a better way.

The entrepreneurs who disrupt industries, the scientists who overturn theories, and the artists who create new movements all practice variations of the same principle. They see where conformity fails, choose their battles carefully, act with intention, and diverge radically from what came before.

This isn't about making you an entrepreneur, revolutionary, or artist. It's about recognizing that the same pattern of thoughtful defiance can apply to any area where the status quo falls short, including your own life.

Many of the stories in the following chapters are extreme. That's by design. They're meant to stretch your sense of what's possible, not to suggest only bold acts pass the test. Rational Defiance also lives in the small, quiet choices we make every day.

You don't need to start a movement or reinvent an industry to defy the status quo. Sometimes, defiance is as subtle as asking a better question, challenging a lazy assumption, or walking away from a commitment that no longer fits. Every small act of defiance chips away at the invisible weight of conformity. They sharpen your instincts. They stretch your courage. Slowly, they built a different way of living.

FROM PHILOSOPHY TO PRACTICE

In this chapter, I've outlined the principles that make defiance rational rather than reckless: pursuing what's better, choosing battles wisely, acting with awareness, and being willing to stand apart.

Understanding these principles is just the beginning. This chapter is the first part of building a foundation for Rational Defiance.

The remaining Mindset chapters—See Clearly, Seek Radical Inputs, and Sample Unconventional Experiences—deepen your capacity to think and live beyond conformity. You'll learn to question what others accept, expand your influences beyond the familiar, and test new ideas through real experience. Together with this chapter's principles, they form an ongoing practice of expanding how you see and act in the world. The wider your foundation, the more possibilities you'll recognize for meaningful defiance.

This chapter introduced the philosophy. Now it's time to build your practice.

CHAPTER SIX

See Clearly

FRANCIS CRICK WAS ONE OF THE GREAT SCIENTISTS OF the twentieth century. In 1953, his work with James Watson and others led to one of biology's most significant discoveries: the structure of DNA. Over the next decades, he helped decode the mechanism of protein synthesis and cracked the three-letter nature of the genetic code. After leading a revolution in biology, he turned to consciousness research at the age of sixty, where he helped transform the study of the mind from philosophy into an empirical science.

What makes Crick's achievements more remarkable is how they required him to defy the status quo both in his career and in his scientific ideas.

Crick started his scientific journey late. He was thirty-one when he entered biology, intent on discovering the secret of life. He'd drifted through his twenties with an abandoned physics PhD and years designing mines for the British military. He had no formal training in biology. By every conventional measure, he was too old, too late, and too unqualified to revolutionize our understanding of life.

But Crick didn't accept the common wisdom and didn't float along the path he was on. His skepticism of his personal status quo compelled him to defy the expected path before him. Because he did, as Matt Ridley concludes in his 2006 biography of Crick, he deserved being "bracketed with Galileo, Darwin, and Einstein as one of the greatest scientists of all time."[92]

This same skepticism shaped his approach to his intellectual life. When he entered biology, scientists had already come around to the concept of genes, but they were abstract concepts. Some still clung to a formerly dominant view called "vitalism"—an idea that life's complexity might require special biological principles beyond simple physics and chemistry.

Crick brought a physicist's skepticism to these assumptions and became one of the fiercest opponents of any remaining vitalist thinking. He insisted that life, however complex, must follow the same fundamental physical laws as everything else. This opened the door to a new era of biology where the mechanisms of life could be studied and manipulated at the molecular level. It paved the way for breakthroughs in genetic engineering, biotechnology, and medicine.

Later in his career, skepticism guided his second great pursuit: the nature of consciousness. He rejected mysterianism, which claims the human mind is incapable of understanding consciousness, and dualism, which sees the mind and body as separate categories. Crick believed consciousness, like life, could be explained by physical processes. His work with Christof Koch aimed to pinpoint the neural correlates of consciousness, the brain's systems that generate conscious experience. Their work helped lay the foundation for modern neuroscience's efforts to understand the mind.

Crick defied these limitations through the same method: relentless skepticism. He questioned whether careers really had expiration dates. He questioned whether life required special forces. He questioned whether consciousness was truly unknowable. Where others saw fixed rules—about age, about nature, about knowing our minds—Crick saw assumptions waiting to be tested.

This skepticism was the foundation of his genius. By refusing to accept what everyone "knew," he could see what everyone missed. This is a lesson for all aspiring deviants: to defy the status quo, we must first see it clearly. When you do, you'll recognize its flaws.

RAISE YOUR STANDARDS

Seeing clearly begins with a simple decision: refusing to accept "good enough."

Like Crick rejecting a comfortable but unfulfilling career at thirty-one, Rational Defiance starts when you decide that mediocrity is no longer acceptable. You have to care about improving. Legendary investor Charlie Munger once said, "If you don't care whether you are rational or not, you won't work on it. Then you will stay irrational and get lousy results."[93]

This applies to everything. If you don't care about the truth, you won't question lies. If you don't care about your relationships, you won't examine them critically. If you don't care about your career, you'll settle for mediocrity. Apathy leads to blind acceptance of the status quo. To improve anything, you must care enough to evaluate, question, and demand better.

But caring isn't enough. You also need to embrace the discomfort that comes with seeing things as they really are. Most of us live in a narrow band of acceptable discomfort. We occupy what Chaitanya Charan calls a zone of "comfortable misery."[94]

This is where the Region-Beta Paradox reveals a cruel irony.

Named after a thought experiment by psychologist Daniel Gilbert, it describes how people often recover faster from worse experiences than from milder ones.[95]

Imagine two destinations, A and B. If B is slightly farther than A, you might choose to walk. But if B is far enough away, you'll drive instead and paradoxically arrive faster than if you had walked to the closer destination A. The same principle applies to life: mild discomfort gets tolerated indefinitely, while acute pain forces immediate action.

Consider how this plays out:

- The toxic job that's "not that bad" keeps you trapped for years, while getting fired might propel you toward your dream career.
- The mediocre relationship persists because it's "fine," while a dramatic breakup forces you to raise your standards.
- The slight health concern gets ignored, while a serious diagnosis sparks transformation.

We're wired to avoid discomfort, but this instinct backfires. By tolerating "just okay," we never experience the productive discomfort that drives real change.

The rationally defiant don't wait for external pain to drive the change. They raise their standards deliberately and refuse to settle.

Fred Smith understood this when conceiving FedEx. In the early 1970s, he saw that package delivery was slow and inefficient. While others accepted these limitations as unavoidable, Smith's discomfort with mediocrity drove him to envision overnight delivery. It was an idea that his Yale professor famously gave him a C grade for.

Starting FedEx meant mortgaging his inheritance, maxing

out credit cards, and at one point flying to Las Vegas to gamble the company's last $5,000 (winning $27,000 to pay a fuel bill).[96] In its first three years, FedEx lost $29 million.[97] Most people would have retreated to comfort. But Smith's standards wouldn't allow him to settle: "Leaders get out in front and stay there by raising the standards by which they judge themselves—and by which they are willing to be judged."[98]

Rational deviants don't just tolerate discomfort—they invite it. Not masochistically but strategically. They understand the path to clarity runs straight through the uncomfortable territory most people spend their lives avoiding. They are willing to see reality without the comfortable filters we usually apply:

- The gap between who you are and who you pretend to be
- The excuses you've used to avoid growth
- The ways you've settled for less than you're capable of
- The comfortable lies you've told yourself

The deeper truth is you're already uncomfortable. The status quo creates its own suffering—the dull ache of unfulfilled potential, the nagging sense you're capable of more, the quiet desperation Thoreau warned about.[99] You can choose the productive discomfort of growth or the deadening discomfort of stagnation.

The only comfortable option is self-deception. And once you've decided to see clearly, that's no longer on the table.

USE FIRST PRINCIPLES

Wanting better isn't enough. You need to understand what "better" actually means. This is where first-principles thinking transforms good intentions into a way of thinking. Most people accept the world as it is. They understand new things by comparing them to what they already know. We reason by analogy. It's a shortcut that blinds us to simple truths.

I witnessed this firsthand when we conducted online surveys. Experienced researchers who joined our team designed digital questionnaires, just as they would for face-to-face interviews. With long conversational introductions, question formats that are impossible on screens, and forty-five-minute interview lengths. They created "paperless" paper surveys, completely missing what digital could do: dynamic question formats, real-time validation, and adaptive interviewing. It's reasoning by analogy at its worst: forcing old limitations into new frameworks.

What was really required was asking more fundamental questions about what we are trying to achieve and what these tools are capable of.

This is first-principles thinking: understanding the core truths to build up your understanding. It has ancient roots dating back to Aristotle believed that true knowledge comes from grasping the first causes and principles of things—understanding why something must be the way it is, and knowing it could not be otherwise.[100] This way of thinking is the basis of many of the most radical innovations and discoveries.

Take the Wright Brothers. At the turn of the twentieth century, aspiring aviators were held back by analogy. They studied birds and tried to replicate their wing-flapping motion.[101] Samuel Langley, backed by the Smithsonian and a $50,000 grant, built an elaborate flying machine based on scaling up along this idea. It crashed into the Potomac River.[102]

Meanwhile, the Wright Brothers approached it differently. They focused on fundamental questions:

- What is flight at its core? (Controlled lift and propulsion)
- What do we actually need? (A way to generate lift, thrust, and control)
- How can we test our assumptions? (Build a wind tunnel, test wing shapes)

By thinking from first principles, they realized wings didn't need to flap. They needed to create a pressure differential. This led to the development of fixed-wing design, systematic testing, and ultimately, the first powered flight. They spent $1,000 and changed the world.

Uber is a modern example. Everyone "knew" that taxi systems required medallions and licensing systems, dispatch centers, professional drivers, and regulated pricing. Rather than accept these as requirements, they asked: What does transportation fundamentally need? Someone who wants a ride, someone willing to provide it, and a way to connect them. Everything else was an assumption. The taxi industry called them crazy, then illegal, then unfair. However, by stripping the problem down to its fundamentals, Uber revealed that most "requirements" were actually just traditions.

So how do we apply first-principles thinking to seeing our status quo clearly?

Richard Feynman is a renowned modern exponent of the idea with a remarkably simple approach. The Nobel Prize-winning physicist was troubled by how people learned. He observed, "I don't know what's the matter with people: they don't learn by understanding; they learn by some other way—by rote, or something. Their knowledge is so fragile!"[103]

To combat this, Feynman developed what is now called the Feynman Technique: explaining concepts in simple terms, as if teaching a child. This method forces you to identify gaps in your knowledge and understand ideas at their most fundamental level.

Try explaining your status quo to a ten-year-old. (An imaginary one will do). Pick any area—your job, your daily routine, a belief you hold. If they asked "Why?" to each answer, how many times would you have had to say, "I don't know" or "That's just how it's done"?

Where you stumble, you've found something worth questioning. This is how first-principles thinking cuts through conformity. When you strip away everything except what a child could understand, what remains is clarity.

Suddenly, you see how much of this is artificial: layers of assumption, tradition, and habit piled on top of simple truths.

You realize:

- Most rules are just someone else's solutions to old problems.
- Most limitations are assumptions that haven't been tested.
- Most complexity exists to preserve the status quo.

Rational deviants understand that real progress comes from breaking things down, questioning assumptions, and rebuilding from the ground up. They refuse to settle for fragile knowledge. Instead, they seek to truly understand.

Armed with higher standards and first-principles thinking, you're ready for the final step: extending this clarity to every corner of your life.

APPLY EVERYWHERE

We've all had moments where we glimpse the flaws in our status quo and suddenly see a part of our life with uncomfortable clarity.

The financially stable job that is draining the life from us. The long-held belief is flat-out wrong. A relationship that is a comfortable prison. These are powerful moments of clarity that create an urgency to change.

And that's where most of us stop. We don't take the next step: questioning the rest of our status quo. If one part of your life is lacking, why assume everything else is solid? Rational Defiance starts with the realization that nothing should be accepted without scrutiny. Seeing the world clearly means being more widely skeptical of all parts of your status quo.

Real change begins when one doubt triggers another. Francis Crick showed this pattern early. As a twelve-year-old, he encountered scientific facts that contradicted what he'd been taught to accept. His response revealed a skeptical mind already forming, "And if some of the Bible is manifestly wrong," he later wrote in his memoirs, "why should any of the rest of it be accepted automatically?"[104]

The lesson is not about rejecting faith but recognizing a fundamental principle: if part of any accepted truth proves false, everything connected to it deserves scrutiny. One thread pulled honestly can unravel an entire fabric of assumptions.

Consider Rachel Carson, who, like Crick, seemed an unlikely revolutionary. She was a marine biologist and nature writer, not an activist. In the 1950s, she was studying the ocean's mysteries and crafting poetic prose about the sea.

Then she noticed something troubling: DDT, a widely used pesticide, was wiping out bird populations. A simple observation—fewer birds in treated areas led her to dig deeper.

Her research revealed a massive, overlooked problem. The unchecked use of synthetic chemicals was harming wildlife, poisoning ecosystems, and endangering human health. Her investigation cascaded into *Silent Spring*, published in 1962. It sparked national debate, challenged the chemical industry, and led to policy changes, including the creation of the Environmental Protection Agency.

Carson's journey shows how a single doubt, properly pursued, can unravel an entire system of false assumptions. Like Crick, she understood that finding one flaw means everything connected deserves examination.

Every breakthrough in science, business, society, and personal life starts with someone willing to pull that first thread and keep pulling:

If this relationship is unfulfilling, what about my other connections?

If this career path was chosen for the wrong reasons, what other life decisions did I inherit rather than choose?

If this belief proved false, what other "truths" have I never examined?

If this habit hurts me, what other routines am I mindlessly repeating?

Each question leads to another, creating a cascade of examination. Not because they're cynics who doubt everything but because they've learned that our assumptions travel in packs. One unexamined assumption usually signals more of them nearby.

This cascade effect is what transforms a moment of clarity into a life of clarity. Pull one thread and watch what else comes loose.

Skepticism rarely reveals the truth in one dramatic revelation but through the patient practice of following each doubt to its conclusion.

SEEING WHAT NO ONE ELSE SEES

We celebrate the outcome of Rational Defiance: the new idea, the artistic creation, the disruptive business. But we don't appreciate enough how these deviants could spot something that needed fixing that no one else did.

Francis Crick's achievements began with him seeing what others couldn't—or wouldn't—see. When he raised his standards, he refused to drift through an unfulfilling physics career. That discomfort with mediocrity gave him the courage to start over at thirty-one.

His intellectual method was one of first-principles thinking, which stripped away mystical explanations and rebuilt understanding from fundamental truths. Where others saw special "vital forces," he saw chemistry and physics.

Then came the cascade. From the origin of life to the nature of the mind, Crick applied his clear-seeing lens everywhere. Each breakthrough revealed new assumptions to question.

These three practices work as a system that is useful to all of us. Standards create the motivation. First principles provide the method. And applying them everywhere ensures you don't stop at comfortable half-truths.

But seeing clearly is just the beginning. You need inputs that stretch your sense of what's possible. Because Rational Defiance is about what can be improved and *how*. For these answers, we need to look beyond our current reality and discover the ideas, people, and places that expand our conception of what is possible. Rational Defiance emerges when a clear-seeing mind encounters radical new perspectives.

CHAPTER SEVEN

Seek Radical Inputs

FRANCIS CRICK WASN'T A CLOSE-MINDED CYNIC. ANOTHER theme in his life was an openness to radical ideas.

In 1973, he and Leslie Orgel proposed "directed panspermia"—the hypothesis that an advanced alien civilization might have intentionally seeded life on Earth.[105] This wasn't the rambling of a crackpot. It was a serious scientist considering an extraordinary explanation for an extraordinary problem: the origin of life. While many dismissed the idea, Crick argued that all possibilities deserved consideration when addressing profound questions. This balance of fierce skepticism paired with radical openness defined his approach everywhere.

He spent hours reading papers others considered pointless or irrelevant. When questioned why, he simply said, "There might be a clue in it."[106]

One of those "clues" came from physicist Erwin Schrödinger's *What Is Life?*—a book outside mainstream biology that helped inspire Crick's pursuit of DNA's structure. By refusing to limit his inputs to conventional sources, Crick found insights others had missed.

He was known for entertaining foolish notions in scientific discussions, believing that any logically consistent idea might open a path to discovery. As he once warned, "The dangerous man is the one who has only one idea, because then he'll fight and die for it."[107]

This captures a critical insight for Rational Defiance. Skepticism alone isn't enough. It reveals only what's wrong with the status quo. To find what could be better, we need a radical curiosity.

Most of us do the opposite. We're skeptical of new ideas while defensive about our current reality. We protect our beliefs instead of expanding them. Most of us live in intellectual bubbles without realizing it. We read the same types of books, follow similar news sources, and have conversations that reinforce what we already believe. We create lives with minimal variation. When all our influences point in the same direction, we mistake that narrow view for the whole picture. We can't imagine alternatives because we've never encountered them.

This chapter is about breaking that pattern. You'll learn how to deliberately seek unconventional inputs through diverse ideas, people, and places.

As Crick showed, breakthrough thinking requires both the courage to question everything and the curiosity to explore anywhere. One without the other leaves you either cynical or naive. Together, they create the conditions for genuine discovery.

EXPLORE DIVERSE IDEAS

Most of us are trapped in an echo chamber where the same ideas are repeated and reinforced. Tendencies like confirmation bias make us seek out ideas that "prove" what we already believe.

Going against this tendency requires effort. The formula to

apply this is simple to articulate, even if it is hard to apply: get exposed to more diverse ideas.

The problem isn't that we don't consume enough information. (It's easy to consume a lot of the same ideas.) It's that we don't get exposed to enough new ideas.

Francis Crick read "pointless" papers because he searched for clues to solve the mysteries of life and consciousness. He understood that the more diverse information he was exposed to, the greater the range of ideas he could draw from. He read everything from physics papers to crystallography studies, seeking clues wherever they might hide.

This same lesson applies to any quest to answer a well-defined problem. If you want to improve your habits, you need to explore the habits of others to understand how they managed their results. If you want to improve your business, you must study the various models other operators have applied.

This directed search for alternatives helps us move beyond seeing the present solution as the only one. It allows us to see the alternatives to the status quo that we may otherwise miss.

But finding solutions to problems isn't the only time we should be curious about new ideas. In a 2017 interview with psychologist Adam Grant, film director Christopher Nolan explained his approach to being open to new ideas:

> If you're going to write, you want to read a lot before you write, without any purpose. I love watching TV, love watching movies, preferably with no sense of purpose. Just being open to things that might inspire you—and staying open.[108]

Writer David Epstein reflected on this purposeless exploration and came away with this conclusion:

Nolan reads "without any purpose." I would argue, though, that there is a purpose in that: to find something that stimulates you but that you couldn't have known to look for.[109]

This is exactly the insight we struggle to grasp in our default state of conformity. Exploring "without purpose" feels haphazard, a stage of mental wandering through ideas that may turn out to be useless or wrong. But they often lead to ideas we didn't even know to look for.

The lesson is to be both an archer and an explorer. Sometimes you need targeted learning aimed at specific problems. Other times, you need to wander through intellectual territories just to see what's there. One approach finds solutions to problems you know. The other finds problems you didn't know existed—and possibilities you never imagined.

Most of us are too rigid in our information diet. We either consume only what's immediately "useful," or we mindlessly scroll through whatever the algorithm serves. Neither builds the diverse mental library that Rational Defiance requires.

Instead, deliberately vary your inputs. Read outside your field. Watch documentaries on topics you know nothing about. Follow thinkers who make you uncomfortable. The purpose is not to accept everything but to expand what you're capable of imagining.

Breakthroughs rarely come from expected sources. They come from the collision of ideas that weren't supposed to meet.

LEARN FROM DIVERSE PEOPLE

As independently minded as Francis Crick was, he wasn't a lone genius who worked in isolation. As Matt Ridley explains:

Crick's intellectual technique, throughout his life, was a dyadic pairing, a long-running two-way conversation with a chosen friend, somewhere between an interrogation and a Socratic dialogue.[110]

Francis Crick constantly sought out collaborators who could challenge him and expand his perspective. He is far from the only great achiever who followed this strategy.

In 1727, at the age of twenty-one, Benjamin Franklin and several friends formed the Junto—or Leather Apron Club—a small group of tradesmen and artisans who met on Friday evenings to discuss morals, politics, and philosophy. Franklin prepared a set of questions to guide their conversations, such as:[111]

- Have you met with anything in the author you last read, remarkable, or suitable to be communicated to the Junto?
- Do you know of any fellow citizen who has lately done a worthy action, deserving praise and imitation? Or who has committed an error proper for us to be warned against and avoid?
- What happy effects of temperance, prudence, moderation, or of any other virtue?

Their debates, Franklin wrote, were to be conducted "in the sincere spirit of inquiry after truth, without fondness for dispute, or desire of victory."[112]

Of course, Franklin's remarkable and varied achievements as an inventor, scientist, writer, and statesman can't be attributed solely to his habit of seeking out diverse perspectives. But it hints at the outlook required to achieve remarkably unconventional results.

Seeking out diverse people with a deliberately open intent to learn is a fundamental habit of rationally defiant individuals. And it is the exact opposite of how most of us build our social circles. We gravitate toward people who think like us, who confirm our biases, who make us comfortable. Our networks, both physical and digital, become echo chambers of agreement. We mistake consensus for truth and comfort for connection.

The same can be said for our professional circles. Most "networking" events, mastermind groups and the like, bring similar people together. Marketers attend these groups to learn from other marketers on, well, marketing. Where are the examples of modern Junto clubs? Where are the places where artists learn from scientists, writers from engineers, entrepreneurs from philosophers? If they exist, I haven't found them. So where do we start?

The most obvious interpretation of this advice is to physically meet other people. To regularly plan interactions with people in different careers, from different backgrounds, with different skills and experiences.

Fortunately, 300 years after the founding of the Junto club, proximity is no longer a barrier to meeting interesting people. Start where you are.

Expand your definition of "meeting." With a growing number of digital ways to connect, a diverse range of perspectives is more accessible than ever before. This advice also extends to "meeting" people through observation. The number of diverse lives captured in biographies is an endless source of ideas and behaviors to study and learn from. You'll never get to actually meet some of the most interesting people in the world who are alive but out of reach or long since deceased. But in most cases, their lives and ideas are available to those curious enough to explore them.

Seek intellectual friction. Join groups where you're not the smartest person in the room. Engage with people whose life experiences differ radically from yours. If you're a technologist, spend time with artists. If you're liberal, have genuine conversations with conservatives.

Ask better questions. Instead of "How was your weekend?" try Franklin's approach, "What have you read lately that changed your thinking?" or "What belief have you reconsidered recently?"

The goal isn't to collect contacts or build a network. It's to find people who make you think differently. As entrepreneur Jim Rohn put it, "You are the average of the five people you spend the most time with."[113] But that's not very useful if all five agree on everything.

So the next time your group concludes that great minds think alike, get worried. The greatest minds aren't like-minded; they're open-minded.

VISIT NEW PLACES

Mark Twain's extensive travels greatly influenced his life and writing and led him to the following conclusion:

> Travel is fatal to prejudice, bigotry and narrow-mindedness, and many of our people need it sorely on these accounts. Broad, wholesome, charitable views of men and things can not be acquired by vegetating in one little corner of the earth all one's lifetime.[114]

No single act changes your status quo more radically than traveling outside your little corner of the world.

Visiting new places means meeting new people, encountering new ideas, and observing systems that are unusual to you as they are normal to those living there. It makes you aware of other versions of reality removed from your own.

Yet most of us confine ourselves to a very limited set of environments: our physical environments, where we live, work, and play, and our digital environments, where we network, socialize, and get our information. But the more limited your environment, the more limited your perspective.

When we travel, it is mainly for "business or pleasure" but rarely for growth and discovery. Of course, we want to travel more, but who has the time?

The idea of travel as a lengthy expedition to some far-off place is part of the problem. Packing up to explore for weeks or months isn't practical for most of us.

But we don't need to spend months and years traveling like Twain, Hemingway, or Bourdain to reap these benefits. A brief visit can be just as enlightening.

Artist and author Julia Cameron created the concept of the "Artist Date," a practice of regularly taking time to explore new environments and experiences alone, purely for inspiration and creative renewal. As she explains in her book *The Listening Path*:

> The Artist Date is the tool of attention. It has two differing emphases: "artist" and "date." Put simply, an Artist Date is a once-weekly solo expedition to do something that enchants or interests you. It is half artist and half date. You are "wooing" your artist. Planned ahead of time—hence "date"—this weekly adventure is something to look forward to. As with a romantic date, anticipation is half the fun.[115]

The features of the *Artist Date*: (1) a regular planned trip, (2) to a place you wouldn't usually visit, (3) with the intent to find inspiration, are applicable everywhere. Artist dates aren't just for artists. Everyone can benefit from a weekly outing to find inspiration.

Starting is simple. Cameron's advice is to ask, "What sounds like fun?" She calls these exercises "assigned play" and reminds her students that "The lists are for giddy delights—nothing serious here. This is not the time to undertake edifying adult pleasures, such as the computer course you've been meaning to take."[116]

With the pressure off, her students' lists take form: visiting a children's bookstore, pet shop, art supply store, the zoo, a fabric store, or attending a play or movie.

Some of these might make your list, but it's easy to come up with your own. Just follow your curiosity, brainstorm with a friend, or ask ChatGPT. Keep it fun, do it regularly, and get inspired.

What's there to discover in these excursions was best said by John Steinbeck: "People don't take trips—trips take people."[117]

REMAIN CRITICAL

There are three important conditions to apply this advice successfully.

First, seek the genuinely radical. Even with the best intentions, it's easy not to stretch ourselves far enough. The business book that confirms your management style. The documentary that validates your worldview. The people who are different but not *that* different.

Our tendency to gravitate to the familiar is a powerful force. We are naturally drawn to ideas, people, and environments that align with our existing beliefs and experiences. So, even when we take up the challenge to venture into uncharted territory, we often stay too close to home. To truly expand our horizons, we must seek out the unfamiliar, unconventional, and even radical and weird.

It means ideas that make you question fundamental assumptions. People who see the world through completely alien lenses. Places that operate by entirely different rules. If you're not occasionally thinking "this is insane," you're not pushing far enough.

Second, prioritize quality information. The internet is full of ideas. Most of it is terrible. Finding radical ideas doesn't mean filling up on influencer advice, clickbait, and soundbites. Instead, seek well-researched and thoughtful perspectives to ensure the insights you gather are valuable. One useful shortcut is to consider how long it took the person to form their ideas. Books and research papers take years to write, essays weeks, and tweets take minutes. It's not a perfect system, but it's a start.

This doesn't mean ignoring all quick content. But treat it as inspiration, not the last word. A viral thread might spark curiosity, but follow it to the source. Find the research paper behind the headline. Read the thinker's book, not just their quotes. Quality inputs offer insights that compound rather than evaporate.

Third, remain critical. As one of my favorite sayings goes, "keep an open mind—but not so open that your brain falls out." Exposure isn't endorsement. You can learn from ideas you ultimately reject.

This is where the balance from earlier chapters matters. Your skepticism prevents you from becoming a naive collector of every wild theory. Your curiosity prevents you from dismissing ideas just because they challenge your worldview. Together, they create productive tension.

The goal isn't to become a contrarian who rejects mainstream thought or a sponge who absorbs every alternative view. It's about building a practice of intelligent exploration—radical enough to expand your boundaries, of high quality to be worth your time, and critical enough to integrate what serves you while discarding what doesn't.

EXPAND YOUR OVERTON WINDOW

A while ago, I saw a tweet that read:

> I love that AC/DC was generally considered super rebellious at one point, and now their music is literally being used in Applebee's commercials.[118]

What seems radical in one era becomes mundane in the next. This isn't just true for rock music—it's how all change happens.

The Overton Window visualizes the range of ideas society considers acceptable at any given time. Inside the window: reasonable, permissible, discussable. Outside: radical, unthinkable, dangerous. But windows shift. Women's suffrage, interracial marriage, remote work, cannabis legalization—all sat outside the window until they didn't.

Here's the crucial insight: we each carry our own personal Overton Window. Just as society has boundaries for acceptable thought, so do we. Our window defines what we consider reasonable, permissible, and normal.

And most of us live with windows far too narrow.

This chapter has been about deliberately expanding that window. When you expose yourself to radical ideas, you discover that reasonable ideas exist outside of what you've encountered before. When you learn from diverse people, you see how different lives can be lived. When you visit new places, you realize how arbitrary your "normal" really is.

Think about your life ten years ago. What would you have said was impossible that you now consider normal? Work remotely? Start a business? Change careers? Leave a relationship? Each expansion of your personal window made new actions possible.

This chapter is about looking ahead. Every input you seek—every radical idea entertained, every diverse person engaged, every new place explored—stretches your window a little wider. And with a wider window comes a richer set of possibilities for who you might become and what you might create.

But possibility alone isn't enough. Ideas must become experiences, which brings us to the next chapter: how to move from collecting inputs to actually experimenting with the futures you can now imagine.

CHAPTER EIGHT

Sample Unconventional Experiences

IN 1974, A TWENTY-YEAR-OLD COLLEGE DROPOUT SPENT months learning calligraphy from a Trappist monk. While his peers were preparing for careers, he was learning about serif typefaces.

Steve Jobs later explained why: "I learned about serif and sans-serif typefaces, about varying the amount of space between different letter combinations, about what makes typography great. It was beautiful, historical, artistically subtle, in a way that science can't capture. And I found it fascinating."[119]

Other than following his interest, it seemed pointless. As he recalled in his famous Stanford commencement speech, "None of this had even a hope of any practical application in my life."[120]

But ten years later, Jobs used that "useless" knowledge to revolutionize computer design. The first Mac introduced typography to personal computing with multiple fonts, proportional spacing, and beautiful text. "If I had never dropped in on that single course in college, the Mac would have never had multiple typefaces or proportionally spaced fonts. And since Windows just copied the Mac, it's likely that no personal computer would have them."[121]

Jobs didn't take that calligraphy class because he foresaw its future value. As he put it, "You can't connect the dots looking forward. You can only connect them looking backwards, so you have to trust that the dots will somehow connect in your future."[122]

However, his example demonstrates how unconventional experiences can create unconventional opportunities.

This chapter is about deliberately creating defiant opportunities through experimentation. Skepticism helps you see the world clearly. Radical inputs reveal alternatives. But it's not enough to admire unconventional paths without walking them. It's easy to collect ideas and never test them. Rational Defiance requires us to build up diverse experiences.

You can read about a new career forever, or you can dabble in it and find out. You can be fascinated by unconventional work schedules or try them and learn. You can theorize about what life would be like without social media, or you can delete your accounts for a month and experience it. You can wonder if you're creative, or you can commit to making something, anything, this week.

The choice is simple: keep wondering or find out. Stay in contemplation or move to experimentation. It is in that gap between thinking and doing that conventional people become capable of unconventional results.

RUN LIFE EXPERIMENTS

Most of us treat decisions as irreversible. Choose a career, and you're locked in for decades. Starting a relationship and backing out means failure. Move to a new city, and you better make it work. This pressure for permanence paralyzes us. So we stick with the familiar rather than risk a "mistake." We've been taught that "real" adults make decisions and see them through. We fall into the trap of consistency, believing that persistence equals virtue.

This resistance intensifies because we underestimate our capacity for change. Psychologists refer to this as the "end of history" illusion. A 2013 study by Quoidbach, Gilbert, and Wilson revealed something startling: while people acknowledge they've changed significantly over the past decade, they consistently predict minimal change in the future.[123]

The thirty-year-olds predicted less change ahead than the forty-year-olds reported experiencing. The forty-year-olds predicted stability while the fifty-year-olds looked back on a decade of transformation. At every age, people believed their current self was the final version.

This illusion makes us overly precious about our choices. If this is who you'll always be, then every decision better be perfect. Every commitment becomes a life sentence. Every experiment risks defining you forever.

But the data shows otherwise. You will change. Your preferences will shift. Your values will evolve. The career that fulfills you at twenty-five might drain you at thirty-five. The lifestyle you crave at forty might bore you at fifty. Treating decisions as permanent when change is guaranteed is a recipe for future misery.

That's why we need another way to view the course of our lives: life is a series of experiments.

This is both a more accurate description of how life really works and a more effective prescription for how we should approach it. You're not the same person who made decisions five years ago, and you won't be the same person five years from now. So why pretend otherwise?

Experiments are attempts to try things to see what happens. It's a bias for testing and learning. It enables us to adapt and grow based on real-world feedback, not just on our preconceptions. Some experiments you'll extend. Others you'll end. None define you permanently.

This is especially crucial for Rational Defiance. Conformity thrives on the illusion of permanence. "This is how things are done" only works if you believe things can't be done differently. "Stay in your lane" only makes sense if lanes are fixed.

When you see life as a series of experiments, you gain permission to test alternatives. That corporate job isn't your identity; it's a current experiment in one way of working. Your social group isn't sacred; it's one among many you might evolve into. Those inherited beliefs aren't permanent fixtures; they're hypotheses awaiting testing.

Every conformist pressure loses its power when you add two words: "for now."

This is how you work...for now.

This is what you believe...for now.

This is who you are...for now.

Because the biggest risk isn't running the wrong experiment. It's pretending your current experiment is your only option.

TAKE MORE SHOTS

Ralph Waldo Emerson agreed that "All life is an experiment" and offered this important extension: "The more experiments you make the better."[124]

On his Substack, David Epstein writes about a strategy he calls "pour out lesser ideas to get to the great ones." Because, as he writes, "creativity research has found that eminent creators just generate more ideas—many of them not so great...Thomas Edison held more than a thousand patents (and was rejected for many more), most completely unimportant."[125] And later, "Two of my favorite writers—Haruki Murakami and Martin McDonagh—have written some of the best and worst stuff I've ever read. One of my favorite artists, sculptor Rachel Whiteread, was the first woman ever to win the Turner Prize...and also the 'Anti-Turner Prize' for the worst British artist. And she won them in the same year."[126]

This principle extends beyond creative work. The most successfully defiant people try a lot and fail a lot. We believe successful people had one bold idea that worked perfectly. We don't see their pile of failed experiments.

We stay trapped because we're trying to get it right the first time.

But the math of experimentation is forgiving. If you try one alternative to the conventional path, you have a slight chance of success. Try five? The odds improve. Try ten? You're almost certain to discover something that works.

If you only get one shot at being different, the stakes feel impossibly high. But when you're running ten experiments, any single failure becomes data, not disaster.

David Epstein concludes that "Creativity is high variance, and your best ideas probably don't come right away."[127] The same is true of defiance. There are many ways to be wrong when you try something different. But that's okay. As Edison noted, "I have not failed. I've just found 10,000 ways that won't work."[128] Every new attempt is one more chance to discover a new defiant success.

GIVE UP EASILY

The consistency trap is the enemy of experimentation. Yet, if you take on many new and unconventional experiences, you'll find some more pleasant, rewarding, or fitting than others. This isn't failure; it's data. And when you realize "this isn't for me," the rational response is to move on to the next experiment, not to persist out of stubbornness.

Charlie Munger understood this when he said, "Most books I don't read past the first chapter. I'm not burdened by bad books."[129]

Inspired by this approach, finance writer Morgan Housel developed his reading strategy of "Lots of Inputs and a Strong Filter," which means to "start as many books as I can but finish few of them."[130] The logic behind this strategy was his realization that "most books don't need to be read to the end, but some books can change your life."[131]

This same principle applies to every experiment you undertake. Most ideas and experiments lead nowhere, but some can transform everything. The key is to try many and abandon them quickly when they don't resonate.

This plays out in every domain. Whether it's the career experiment, the pottery class, or the 5:00 a.m. routine—if the experiment doesn't succeed, quitting is wise, not weak. You've learned something valuable about yourself without wasting months or years on the wrong path.

The traditional view would have you persist, believing struggle builds character. But there's a crucial difference between productive struggle and pointless suffering. When learning a musical instrument, the initial difficulty is part of the journey. When trapped in a career that drains you, the difficulty serves no purpose except to delay your search for something better. This approach requires distinguishing between two types of discomfort:

1. **Initial friction:** The natural discomfort of trying something new. This often fades as competence grows. Give experiments enough time to move past this phase, where you know enough to call the result.
2. **Fundamental misalignment:** A deeper recognition that this path conflicts with your values, strengths, or vision. This intensifies rather than fades with time. When you feel this, trust it.

The fear, of course, is we jump from one thing to another without ever developing mastery. But remember, the goal isn't to quit everything. It's to quit the wrong things quickly so you can pour yourself into the right ones fully. The startup culture mantra of "fail fast, fail cheap" applies here too.

It's time to give up on "never giving up" as a blanket philosophy. Strategic quitting is how you find what's worth persisting in. In a world that glorifies grinding through any obstacle, sometimes the most defiant act is simply walking away.

IMITATE FIRST

To become authentically defiant, you must first become a skilled imitator.

That seems wrong. Isn't imitation the opposite of originality? How can we be authentic when we copy others?

It turns out this fear of imitation is unfounded. Original work doesn't appear out of nowhere. It starts with an existing model and then transforms into something unique. William Zinsser understood this when he advised writers:

> Never hesitate to imitate another writer. Imitation is part of the creative process for anyone learning an art or a craft. Bach and

Picasso didn't spring full-blown as Bach and Picasso; they needed models. This is especially true of writing. Find the best writers in the fields that interest you and read their work aloud. Get their voice and their taste into your ear—their attitude toward language. Don't worry that by imitating them you'll lose your own voice and your own identity. Soon enough you will shed those skins and become who you are supposed to become.[132]

This is true for all of us. Creating novel work is initially a process of discovery and imitation. There are many famous examples of this idea in action.

Steve Jobs studied the innovations of Xerox and then transformed them into the groundbreaking Macintosh. J. K. Rowling built upon the tradition of British boarding school novels to create the magical world of Harry Potter. Pablo Picasso initially mastered classical techniques before pioneering the Cubist movement. The Beatles emulated American rock and roll before evolving into their iconic sound. Maya Angelou absorbed the styles of classic poets and then crafted her powerful literary voice.

Zinsser's advice to "get their voice in your ear" can be taken a step further. We shouldn't just passively expose ourselves to ideas, methods, and styles, but we should also experience them through imitation. Again, an analogy from writing illustrates the point.

Hunter S. Thompson, pioneer of Gonzo journalism and one of America's most distinctive literary voices, understood this deeply. As a young writer, he didn't just read Fitzgerald—he typed out *The Great Gatsby* word for word. "He wanted to know what it felt like to write a masterpiece," Johnny Depp later explained.[133]

Through this radical act of imitation, Thompson internalized the rhythm, structure, and flow of great prose. The same writer who later broke every rule of journalism first learned those rules by copying them verbatim. The result? One of the most original voices in American literature emerged from deliberate imitation.

The principle of experimentation in life and business follows the same logic. Be led by your curiosity to discover the ideas, habits, and methods of others. Copy them as an experiment. Soon enough, you'll find your unique path and perspective.

Never be afraid to imitate first.

DON'T IMAGINE, FIND OUT

Experimentation is the way to test your imagination.

We're all experts at imagining alternative lives. The entrepreneur visualizes building a company while sitting in their cubicle. The would-be artist pictures gallery openings during their commute. The aspiring minimalist mentally declutters while surrounded by possessions.

This passive imagination is conformity's best friend. It gives us the satisfaction of considering change without the discomfort of attempting it. The gap between imagining and experiencing is vast.

For several years in my early twenties, I planned to enter academia. I imagined all the things I would enjoy about the experience: conducting interesting research, teaching eager students, and dedicating my life to intellectual growth.

But as I completed my Master's in psychological research, I got an opportunity to do a one-year internship at a marketing research agency. I needed practical experience for my accreditation, so I thought why not try it for a year? I could always return to my academic path. Plus, I was guest lecturing at universities during this time, so I could test both paths simultaneously.

That decision to experiment for a year in a field I hadn't known existed six months before changed the course of my life.

After a while, I found lecturing tedious. Preparing lectures and presenting them didn't give me the satisfaction I'd imagined. Since this part of academic life far outweighed the time I would spend on research and writing, I couldn't see myself making a career this way.

My one-year experiment in market research also delivered surprising results. I had low expectations going into it. I had never wanted to work in a corporate environment. Yet I found that work enjoyable and discovered I was good at it.

Two years after starting my market-research experiment, a fellow intern and I decided to strike out on our own. At the age of twenty-four, we started Columinate. Starting and growing that business was a formative part of my life and has provided me with opportunities I never imagined when this journey started, all because I took a chance and experimented.

I'd imagined two different paths. I was wrong about both.

This pattern shows up everywhere. The corporate executive imagines entrepreneurship as pure freedom, only to discover they're trading one set of constraints for another. The city dweller pictures rural life as peaceful simplicity, then confronts isolation and inconvenience. The employee dreams of remote work as paradise and then struggles with boundaries and loneliness.

The lesson isn't that our dreams are wrong. It's that imagination alone can't reveal what's right. No amount of planning, thinking, and fantasizing can replace the data of direct experience. You discover that some rebellions aren't worth it. Others are more valuable than you'd hoped. But you only learn by doing.

So take the class. Start the side project. Spend a week living that different life. No amount of imagination can replace the clarity of experience. And clarity, however uncomfortable, is what Rational Defiance requires.

Part III

The Defiant Path

A DEFIANT MINDSET REVEALS WHAT'S POSSIBLE ON THE other side of the status quo. But thinking differently isn't enough if you don't act. The chapters ahead aren't about quick wins or temporary rebellions. They're about the kind of sustained defiance that reshapes careers, builds movements, creates innovations, or fundamentally transforms how you live. These bigger ambitions—the ones that take months or years to realize—require more than an expanded mindset. They require a vision, a plan, focus, and the courage to stay the course when resistance arrives. You'll discover how to find what you truly stand for, set goals that are actually yours, clear away the distractions that keep you stuck, and maintain your resolve when everyone thinks you're crazy. We start with the most important question of all: what do you stand for?

CHAPTER NINE

Stand for Something

WHAT DO YOU WANT?

Not what you think you should want. Not what others expect you to want. But what do you deeply want—enough to sustain years of defiant action to achieve?

Most of us fumble this question. We offer vague aspirations ("success," "happiness," "making a difference"). Or, more honestly, we admit we just don't know.

It's a universal struggle. The 2004 movie *The Notebook* captured it in a scene that became an internet meme. Noah desperately asks Allie, "What do you want? What do you want?" as she struggles to decide on their future together. Her anguished response—"It's not that simple!"—resonates so strongly because we've all been there.

That's why it's remarkable when someone makes it seem simple.

Bertrand Russell distilled his entire life's purpose into three guiding "passions." He opened his 1956 autobiography with a prologue titled "What I Have Lived For," declaring:

Three passions, simple but overwhelmingly strong, have governed my life: the longing for love, the search for knowledge, and unbearable pity for the suffering of mankind. These passions, like great winds, have blown me hither and thither, in a wayward course, over a deep ocean of anguish, reaching to the very verge of despair.

I have sought love, first, because it brings ecstasy—ecstasy so great that I would often have sacrificed all the rest of life for a few hours of this joy. I have sought it, next, because it relieves loneliness—that terrible loneliness in which one shivering consciousness looks over the rim of the world into the cold unfathomable lifeless abyss. I have sought it, finally, because in the union of love I have seen, in a mystic miniature, the prefiguring vision of the heaven that saints and poets have imagined. This is what I sought, and though it might seem too good for human life, this is what—at last—I have found.

With equal passion I have sought knowledge. I have wished to understand the hearts of men. I have wished to know why the stars shine. And I have tried to apprehend the Pythagorean power by which number holds sway above the flux. A little of this, but not much, I have achieved.

Love and knowledge, so far as they were possible, led upward toward the heavens. But always pity brought me back to earth. Echoes of cries of pain reverberate in my heart. Children in famine, victims tortured by oppressors, helpless old people a hated burden to their sons, and the whole world of loneliness, poverty, and pain make a mockery of what human life should be. I long to alleviate this evil, but I cannot, and I too suffer.

This has been my life. I have found it worth living, and would gladly live it again if the chance were offered me.[134]

I've always found this piece moving, not just for its poetry but for its power. Russell's ideals were simple, profound, and sustained a life at odds with the status quo.

Love led him to defy Victorian morality, championing divorce, openly discussing sexuality, and living through multiple marriages despite the scandal. Knowledge drove him to challenge religious orthodoxy until Cambridge dismissed him, and his peers condemned him. Compassion pulled him to protest war and nuclear weapons, landing him in prison for his pacifism.

Russell's actions, whether challenging marriage norms, questioning religious authority, or protesting war, emerged from something deeper than the act itself. His three passions made every defiant choice meaningful.

This is what most of us miss. We focus on the visible acts of defiance: changing careers, starting movements, breaking habits. We see goals and tactics. But without a deeper foundation, these are random acts of defiance. Everything starts with your foundational ambitions. Or, as Epictetus once said, "In every act observe the things which come first, and those which follow it; and so proceed to the act."[135]

This foundation makes defiance rational. They define what's better. Without knowing what you stand for, you can't judge whether change improves anything. They make you selective. When you know what matters deeply, you stop fighting every battle. They enable deliberate action. Instead of impulsive rebellion, your defiance becomes strategic. And they provide sustained motivation so that when resistance arrives, they remind you why the struggle is worth it.

With something to stand for, you don't constantly decide whether to conform or defy. Your foundational ambitions make that choice for you, again and again.

CREATE YOUR MANIFESTO

Russell's ideals "governed" his life and "blew him hither and thither" against conventional currents. His three passions put him at odds with his world. But they were strong enough for him to stand firm.

That's the difference between a manifesto and a simple list of values. Values tell you what's important. A manifesto declares what you'll fight for. It's inherently defiant. You don't write one to preserve things as they are but to justify why they must change.

The film *Jerry Maguire* captured this perfectly in a scene that my generation will never forget. A successful sports agent, alone in a Miami hotel room, starts typing: "It's 1:00 a.m. and this might be the bad pizza I had earlier talking, but I believe I have something to say. Or rather, I have something to say that I believe in." What follows is twenty-five pages of brutal honesty about what his industry and his life had become:

> Recently, I was asked by the son of a client, in so many words, "What do you stand for?" I was lost for an answer. At 14, I wasn't lost for that answer. At 18, I wasn't lost for an answer. At 35, I was blown away that I had no answer. I could only look at the face of a 12-year-old boy...just looking at me for the answer I didn't have.

By 3:13 a.m., he admits, "I have lost the ability to bullshit."

By 4:45 a.m., he'd found his truth, "Fewer clients. Less dancing. More truth." Not a complex strategy. Not a business plan. Just a clear declaration of what must change. "The secret to this job," he writes, quoting his mentor, "is personal relationships." Everything else—the money, the deals, the "tap dance" of flattery and lies—had buried this simple truth.

By morning, he's photocopied his manifesto and distributed it to his entire agency. Within hours, he's fired. His colleagues think he's lost his mind. But for the first time in years, he knew exactly what he stood for.

Real manifestos chase this same clarity.

Frank Lloyd Wright felt this friction at thirty-eight. Already successful, he felt suffocated by the European imitation dominating American architecture. His 1908 manifesto "In the Cause of Architecture" declared, "Buildings like people must first be sincere, must be true."[136] The whole piece reads less like a work of aesthetic preference and more like a statement of moral conviction. For the next fifty years, when clients wanted conventional Victorian houses, he refused. When critics called his Prairie School strange, he pushed further. Every building that followed became an expression of his ideals, culminating in works like Fallingwater in 1935, a house that not only sits near nature but also cantilevers over it.

Austrian graphic designer Stefan Sagmeister is another example. Every seven years, he closes his successful New York studio for a full year to rediscover what matters. During his 2008 Bali sabbatical, he created "Things I Have Learned in My Life So Far" as massive public installations. "Worrying solves nothing" spelled out in ten thousand bananas. "Complaining is silly. Either act or forget" woven across a valley. These were public declarations against the anxiety and vanity suffocating creative work. Each sabbatical cost him a year of revenue. But they kept him honest. As he explained in his 2009 TED talk, he started because he "had become a robot."[137] His visual manifestos ensure he never becomes one again.

You don't need Jerry's crisis, Russell's eloquence, or Sagmeister's open calendar. You just need the courage to stop bullshitting—especially yourself—about what you stand for and what must change. That gap between what is and what should be is where manifestos are born.

Start with what bothers you most:
What accepted "truth" makes you angry?
What compromise do you make daily that feels like betrayal?
What would you change if you knew you couldn't fail?
What are you pretending not to know?

- **Write without editing.** Jerry Maguire wrote through the night, fueled by coffee and clarity. Follow his example (coffee and late night optional) and just write without self-censoring.
- **Look for patterns in what you write.** What themes keep surfacing? What ideas underlie both your frustration and your hope?

The format doesn't matter. Russell reflected on his in poetic paragraphs. Wright penned a book on architectural philosophy. Sagmeister creates visual installations. Find the form that works for you, and know that your manifesto will evolve. Just like Sagmeister's life lessons change with each sabbatical. Having an imperfect one now is better than none at all.

So write one now. Or at 1:00 a.m., when you have something to say that you believe in. But write one. Find out what you stand for.

FINDING YOUR DEFIANT EDGE

When you write your manifesto, something interesting happens. Not everything that emerges will be defiant. You'll discover ideals that align perfectly with conventional wisdom—wanting meaningful relationships, seeking financial security, valuing health. There's nothing wrong with these. If they're genuinely yours, honor them.

But pay special attention to the other ones. The ideals that make you hesitate before writing them down. The ambitions that seem too bold to admit. The truths that contradict what everyone "knows." These defiant ideals are the most fragile. They're the easiest to edit out, water down, or bury under more acceptable aspirations.

Your conformist ideals will take care of themselves, and the world will support them. But your defiant ambitions need protection. They need to be strengthened, clarified, and pushed even further.

The next sections will help you do exactly that. The biggest risk isn't that your manifesto will be too radical. It's that you'll unconsciously tame it before it has a chance to change anything.

TAKE IT FURTHER

Look again at these defiant ideals. How did you do? Have you taken it far enough? Or have you settled for a watered-down version of what you really believe?

It's hard to dream big when the world expects you to think small. So we declare principles, but they're timid. We stand for something, but it's something small.

As Steve Jobs explained in an interview:

> When you grow up, you tend to get told the world is the way it is and your life is just to live your life inside the world. Try not to bash into the walls too much. Try to have a nice family, have fun, save a little money. That's a very limited life.[138]

But then he added the crucial insight:

> Life can be much broader once you discover one simple fact and that is everything around you that you call life was made up by people that were no smarter than you. And you can change it. You can influence it. You can build your own things that other people can use. Once you learn that, you'll never be the same again.[139]

Life can be much broader once you stop confusing the truly impossible for socially possible.

When Roger Bannister approached the four-minute mile in 1954, experts declared it was physically impossible. The human body, they said, just wasn't built for the feat. Runners had been stuck at 4:01 for nine years. Bannister, a medical student, did his own calculations. He concluded the limit was psychological, not physical. On May 6, 1954, he ran a mile in 3:59.4. Within forty-six days, John Landy broke Bannister's record. Within three years, sixteen other runners had broken the "impossible" barrier.[140] Today, it's the standard for professional middle-distance runners.

This reveals something crucial about what's "impossible." We rarely attempt the impossible like traveling faster than light. But we constantly surrender to the socially impossible. We let our status quo define what we're allowed to imagine.

This matters because your manifesto—what you stand for—becomes the ceiling of your defiance. If your principles are preshrunk to fit acceptable boundaries, your actions will fit in those boundaries. Russell didn't stand for "better relationships" or "more knowledge" or "helping others." His passions were absolute: the longing for love, the search for knowledge, and an unbearable pity for the suffering of mankind. No moderation. No reasonableness. No fingerprints of what others deemed appropriate to want. He was willing to defy whatever stood in the way of pursuing his truths.

There's another myth that kills defiant ambition: that bigger convictions require proportionally more effort. That 10x results demand 10x work.

But there are so many examples that show how wrong this is. The effort to reach further is often the same as aiming for less. Investor Sieva Kozinsky shared this lesson he received from a mentor in his twenties:

> It takes just as much time to build a small business, as a big business. You may as well build a big business.[141]

Everything I learned from growing a startup says this is right. I worked just as hard when the business was smaller than when it was bigger. Settling for a smaller business because it's less work is an illusion.

The same goes for other things. If the effort is similar, you should strive for the more ambitious target. If you plan to study, why not apply to the best schools? If you're going to work forty hours a week, why not aim for more success and fulfillment in a better role? If you're going to spend an hour in the gym, why not increase the pace or weight on the bar in pursuit of better results? If you're going to defy, why not go all the way?

"Be realistic. Start small. Don't overreach." This is exactly backward. The cost of thinking small is you still pay full price in your effort, but you receive a fraction of the potential reward.

This doesn't mean seeking more of what the world defines as success but rather defining it yourself. Every version of your dreams is valid, as long as it's yours. For some, this means building a larger company, creating more, climbing the ladder faster, taking on the biggest project, and making the most significant impact. For others, it means scaling down to create space for other passions, living a slower life, or finding your version of balance amidst many desires. Whatever your ambitions, you need to free your imagination from the constraints that prevent you from fully pursuing them.

When you apply this strategy, those lingering questions won't disappear: Will it work? Can I do it? Is it realistic?

You'll find out soon enough. First, allow yourself to dream.

DON'T EDIT OUT THE DANGER

In 2006, the EDGE Foundation asked 119 leading thinkers a provocative question: "What is your dangerous idea?" The result is one of my favorite books.

The answers were revelatory. Not because they were shocking (though some were) but because they revealed what brilliant minds think when given permission to be intellectually reckless. Psychologist Steven Pinker suggested that groups might differ genetically in their talents and temperaments.[142] Physicist Freeman Dyson proposed that genetic engineering could create new human species.[143] Philosopher Daniel Dennett argued that religion might be a phenomenon that damages its hosts while spreading itself.[144]

These were Nobel laureates, university presidents, and public intellectuals, not cranks or contrarians. But even they needed permission to voice ideas they'd normally keep private. Ideas too radioactive for academic journals. Too nuanced for TED Talks. Too dangerous for polite company.

The word "dangerous" was carefully chosen. Not false ideas that are merely wrong. Not evil ideas. But dangerous ideas: truths that threaten the comfortable consensus, that destabilize accepted wisdom, that make people genuinely uncomfortable because they might be right.

This is what your defiant ideals need to become. Not safe

positions everyone can nod along to but dangerous ambitions that challenge the status quo you're trapped in.

Notice the difference between these two convictions:

"I stand for work-life balance."

"Most careers are elaborate forms of imprisonment where we trade our finite existence for the illusion of security."

Even if you disagree with the second one, notice how it lands differently. The first is a LinkedIn post. The second forces you to confront an uncomfortable possibility. Now imagine believing it—really believing it—and having to navigate a world built on the opposite assumption. That's what a dangerous idea demands.

Look at your manifesto. Where are you still being polite? Where are you hedging? What truth are you softening because it might upset people, including yourself?

The most powerful manifestos contain at least one genuinely dangerous idea. Something that would get you disinvited from dinner parties if you said it out loud. Something that makes even you uncomfortable because it demands so much change.

Don't edit out the danger. That's where transformation begins. Because once you know what you stand for, the next question is "What are you going to do about it?"

CHAPTER TEN

Set Your Course

IN 1970, YVON CHOUINARD TOOK A TRIP TO SCOTLAND TO surf the freezing waters of the North Atlantic. Not exactly what most people do. But Chouinard isn't like most people.

It was on this trip when he stumbled upon a shop where he bought a rugby shirt. It kept him warm, but he also discovered their ideal durability for rock climbing. The thick cotton collar prevented his climbing sling from cutting into his neck.

This was a pivotal moment in the founding story that would ultimately lead to a billion-dollar company. But not in a way the business world would recognize.

When Chouinard returned to California and sold rugby shirts to climbers, he wasn't executing a business plan. He was solving his friends' problems. As sales grew, he faced the same pressure every entrepreneur faces: to set conventional business goals. Scale fast. Maximize profits. Go public. Dominate the market.

Instead, Chouinard asked different questions: How do we grow without destroying what we love? How do we succeed without becoming what we hate?

His goals looked irrational to any business school graduate. He refused to take the company public. He capped growth at a sustainable pace. He ran ads telling people NOT to buy their jackets if they didn't need them. He closed operations for environmental retreats. He let employees leave work to surf when the waves were good.

While other CEOs chased quarterly earnings, Chouinard chased alignment between his business and his ideals. His deeper ambition wasn't conquering markets but protecting wild places.

This was his playbook for decades. Then, in 2022, at age eighty-three, he made one more defiant move. He gave it all away, transferring Patagonia to a trust and nonprofit dedicated to fighting climate change. "One option was to sell Patagonia and donate all the money," he wrote. "But we couldn't be sure a new owner would maintain our values...Another path was to take the company public. What a disaster that would have been...Truth be told, there were no good options available. So, we created our own."[145]

That last line captures everything: when the conventional goals don't fit, create your own. Because the real danger when setting defiant goals isn't what you think.

We all know we struggle to follow through when setting goals. Life gets in the way, motivation fades, and habits return. Frameworks like SMART goals try to solve that by making goals more achievable, and we'll get to that. But deeper down, there are two hidden dangers when setting defiant goals.

First, we set too many goals. We scatter our defiance across dozens of aspirations, ensuring none receive the focus they need to challenge the status quo. When everything matters, nothing does.

Second, we set the wrong goals entirely. Not wrong because

they're too hard or too easy. Wrong because they were never ours to begin with. Even if we pursue them with perfect discipline, we discover we've been climbing someone else's mountain.

Chouinard never aimed for the summit that everyone else was climbing. He picked his own and defined his own route. His goals weren't better or worse than traditional business goals. But they were focused, and they were his.

This chapter is about applying these lessons yourself. Your manifesto is about discovering your destiny. Without it, your goals are just conformity with deadlines. This chapter is about navigation. Turning those grand ambitions into specific plans that are focused enough to matter and authentic enough to sustain you when the path gets steep.

SET GOALS SMARTLY

You've probably heard of SMART goals. Since George Doran introduced the framework in 1981, it's become the universal standard for goal setting. Specific, Measurable, Achievable, Relevant, Time-bound.[146] Every corporate workshop teaches it. Every self-help book preaches it. It helps turn vague hopes into structured plans.

Consider two entrepreneurs:

A sets this goal: "Increase monthly revenue by 20 percent within six months by launching two new product features and hiring three salespeople."

B sets theirs this way: "Build something so useful that customers tell their friends about it without being asked."

The first goal is SMART. It's specific (20 percent increase), measurable (revenue tracking), achievable (with new features and sales), relevant (to business growth), and time-bound (six months). The second is vague (what's "useful?"), hard to measure (how do you track organic word-of-mouth?), unclear if achievable, and has no timeline. Clearly A has a greater chance to succeed.

But for rational deviants, SMART alone isn't enough. It helps you get to your destination, but it doesn't help you choose the right one. It's a system for execution, not for focus or authenticity. To make your defiant ambitions a reality, you need two more criteria:

Limited: You can only defy successfully in a few areas at once. Everything else is strategic conformity or deliberate neglect.

Yours: The goal must emerge from your manifesto, not someone else's playbook.

While Relevant (the R in SMART) and Yours might sound similar, they ask very different questions.

Relevant checks whether a goal fits into your broader plan. If you're a product manager, a goal to improve team velocity is relevant. If you're training for a marathon, running five days a week is relevant. These goals make logical sense in the context of what you're already doing. But *Yours* asks a deeper question: does this align with my manifesto? A promotion might be relevant to your career path. But is your career path consistent with your ambitions? Is that tradeoff yours or just the next thing you're "supposed" to want? Relevant keeps your goals aligned. Yours keeps them honest.

With those two additions, the full framework becomes:

SMARTLY = Specific, Measurable, Achievable, Relevant, Time-bound, Limited, Yours.

The additions of "Limited" and "Yours" change everything. They force trade-offs. They filter out noise. And they ensure that what you're working toward is both doable and worth it.

The real danger isn't setting unrealistic goals. It's setting goals that don't matter and reaching them anyway.

LIMIT RUTHLESSLY

Research in decision science reveals why limiting goals matters for Rational Defiance. When faced with too many choices or goals, we experience what psychologists call "decision fatigue"—our mental resources become depleted, and we default to the path of least resistance.

Studies by Kathleen Vohs and others have shown that making multiple decisions depletes our self-control, leading us to choose the easiest option available.[147] This connects directly to Samuelson and Zeckhauser's findings on status quo bias—when overwhelmed, we're even more likely to stick with whatever already exists.[148] Similarly, Barry Schwartz's research on the "paradox of choice" shows that when overwhelmed with options, people often choose nothing at all—effectively choosing the status quo by default.[149] This is conformity's secret weapon: it doesn't need to convince you to follow along; it just needs to exhaust you until following along is all you have energy for.

In 1896, the Italian economist Vilfredo Pareto observed that a small proportion of people held most of the wealth. Studying income data in Italy, he found that roughly 20 percent of the population owned about 80 percent of the land. He noticed similar patterns elsewhere and modeled the phenomenon mathematically in his Cours d'économie politique. Later thinkers generalized his finding into what's now called the Pareto principle—the idea that a small number of causes often produce most of the results.[150]

This pattern, now called the Pareto Principle, also reveals a truth about goals: a small number creates most of your results. The rest are largely distractions.

This 80/20 rule is remarkably powerful when applied to the right goals. But it is incredibly draining when we ignore it.

Even the best goals will collapse under the weight of too many competing priorities. Defiance requires energy. It takes time and sustained effort to go against the grain. And most people are spread too thin.

That's why successful deviants embrace essentialism: focusing only on what matters and ignoring the rest. It's a form of rebellion. A refusal to play by the rules of more. This focus has to show up in three places: your goals, your choices, and your efforts.

LIMIT GOALS

Most of us set too many goals. Even the best intentions can become noise when there are too many of them. Essentialists recognize this. They ask what's essential and cut the rest.

William Zinsser shares this approach for writers who struggle to simplify what they have to say:

> If you give me an eight-page article and I tell you to cut it to four pages, you'll howl and say it can't be done. Then you'll go home and do it, and it will be much better. After that comes the hard part: cutting it to three.[151]

Warren Buffet once said, "The difference between successful people and really successful people is that really successful people say no to almost everything."

That means saying no to many "good" ideas and goals. In fact, these are the most dangerous. Bad goals are easy to reject. But good-but-not-essential goals? They'll steal your life in small increments.

LIMIT CHOICES

Choices are the options you have to reach your goals. It's easy to come up with several ways to reach them. But having too many options can backfire.

That's the paradox of choice: the more choices we have, the more likely we are to settle for the status quo. This happens because we become overwhelmed when evaluating too many options. So, instead of trying, we avoid the effort and stick to what's familiar.

An essentialist mindset overcomes this by limiting options to increase the quality of our decisions. By focusing only on a limited number of alternatives for every decision, we avoid analysis paralysis and can see the benefit of deviating from the status quo. This applies to any situation where we have many possible options. Essentialists stretch their comfort zones deliberately instead of avoiding choices.

At work, instead of getting overwhelmed with every available project, an essentialist considers only those tasks that align with their long-term career goals. Instead of over-analyzing every new diet trend or fitness regimen, they seek a few simple, sustainable, healthy habits that move them in the right direction. Instead of trying every self-help technique or productivity hack, an essentialist identifies a few key strategies that have a significant impact on their personal growth.

By focusing on fewer choices, we escape the inertia that accompanies choice overload.

LIMIT EFFORTS

Your efforts are the actions you take based on your choices. Like your goals and choices, an excess of actions will derail your plans.

You need to spend more time asking what you should be doing to achieve your goals instead of mindlessly doing as much as you can.

Gary Keller is the founder of Keller Williams, which is the largest real estate company in the world by agent count. In his book *The One Thing,* he advocates for applying a ruthless version of essentialism, focusing only on the most important thing that will get you the results you desire, because, as he explains,

> you can become successful with less discipline than you think, for one simple reason: success is about doing the right thing, not about doing everything right.[152]

Your defiant results, like much else in life, follow a law of disproportionate returns. A small number of your efforts produce almost all your results. The skill is to discover those and go all in while ignoring everything else.

When pursuing your goals, it's worth remembering that you can't break the mold if you're buried under it.

MAKE IT YOURS

In a 1999 study, Sheldon and Elliot showed that when people set goals consistent with their core values and genuine interests, they invest more "sustained effort" and are more likely to achieve those goals. Crucially, attaining these authentic goals led to greater need satisfaction and increased psychological well-being.[153]

Unfortunately, authentic goal-setting is rare. Most of us unconsciously adopt goals that were never ours to begin with.

Consider the ritual of New Year's resolutions. We all set our goals when the calendar changes, regardless of where we are on

January 1. Are you in the middle of a major transition? Overwhelmed with existing commitments? Ready for change, or just following the annual tradition? The arbitrary date doesn't account for your actual circumstances, yet we all dutifully list our intentions because that's when everyone else does it.

More telling is how similar our goals tend to be. Psychologists call this "goal contagion"—we unconsciously copy the ambitions of those around us. Want to lose weight? Save more money? Get promoted? Find love? You're not alone. Research shows these goals are shared by a third to half of Americans.

These are important areas of life, certainly. But the conventional "copy and paste" approach to goal-setting bypasses the harder question: What do *you* uniquely want? Not what sounds good. Not what impresses others. Not what you think you should want. But what actually aligns with your vision for your life.

The danger becomes clear as you approach the finish line. How many people achieve the promotion only to discover it's 50 percent more work for 20 percent more pay? How many reach their fitness goal only to realize the lifestyle is unsustainable? How many build the business, find the relationship, or buy the house, only to wonder, "Is this it?"

We ignore the signals that we're chasing someone else's dream. We persevere because that's what we're told to do. We celebrate the achievement while privately feeling empty.

Andre Agassi spent years as one of the world's top tennis players while harboring a secret: he hated tennis. In his autobiography *Open*, he reveals the truth behind his outward success. His father forced him to hit 2,500 balls a day from age two. The goal was never his. "I play tennis for a living, even though I hate tennis, hate it with a dark and secret passion," he wrote.[154]

At least Agassi had eight Grand Slam titles and millions

in prize money to show for his misery. Most of us chase other people's dreams for far less. We sacrifice our twenties for careers our parents chose, pursue degrees that impress our peers, and climb ladders leaning against the wrong walls—all for a fraction of Agassi's compensation. He found peace only after retiring to pursue his real passion: education philanthropy. But how many of us retire from dreams that were never ours with nothing but regret to show for it?

Goals that are truly yours require honest self-examination. Before committing to any goal, put it through these filters:

- **Does this goal align with my manifesto?** Your manifesto—those deep ambitions you've declared—should be the test for every goal. If you can't draw a clear line from this goal to those core principles, you're probably chasing someone else's definition of success.
- **Which conformity trap might be influencing this choice?** Be ruthless in your assessment. Are you pursuing this to stay consistent with a past version of yourself that no longer exists? Are you aiming here because others expect it of you? Are you limiting yourself to what seems possible in your current environment? Recognition is the first step to resistance.
- **Do I actually want what success looks like?** Imagine you achieve everything this goal promises. The promotion is yours. The weight is lost. The business is built. Does that future excite you or fill you with dread? If the prize at the end doesn't appeal to you, why are you running the race?

Most goals fail this test. They're performance art, meaningful only if others applaud. The promotion that's really about the announcement. The marathon that's really about the Instagram post. The degree that's really about the family's approval.

These questions bring a rare clarity that few of us ever confront. Goals that fail these tests were never really yours. They're borrowed ambitions, inherited expectations, or default options masquerading as personal choices. Pursuing them—even successfully—is just another form of conformity.

TEST THE END

"The trouble with not having a goal," wrote humorist Bill Copeland, "is that you can spend your whole life running up and down the field and never score."[155]

That's the standard case for goal setting; it gives direction. Systems like SMART help you reach your destination efficiently. But efficiency in the wrong direction is still wasted motion.

Here's an exercise worth doing before you commit to any major goal: write two letters from your future self. First, write the resignation letter—why you might walk away:

> I'm quitting because, despite achieving everything—the metrics, the title, the recognition—I've become someone I don't recognize. The success feels hollow because it was never my definition of success.

Then write the renewal letter—why you might go deeper:

> I'm doubling down because this journey revealed who I really am. Every challenge confirmed this is my path. The work energizes rather than drains me. I've become more myself, not less.

Seal or save both letters. Set a reminder for a future date in your pursuit. When you open them, you'll know immediately which one rings true. This isn't about predicting failure but rather creating a compass reading for when you're too deep in the forest to see clearly.

If the resignation letter feels true when you read it, you'll still have time to change course. If the renewal letter resonates, you'll have confirmation you're on your path. Either way, you'll have protected yourself from the worst fate: spending years climbing the wrong mountain and only realizing it at the summit.

Even the right goals, pursued for the right reasons, face a challenge. The path to achievement is littered with distractions accumulated from your past. It's time to clear the way.

CHAPTER ELEVEN

Silence Distractions

AT THE BEGINNING OF THIS YEAR, I FINALLY REVIEWED the subscriptions on my credit card. I discovered fifteen recurring charges for apps, publications, and streaming services. Of those, I used only five. I had been paying, in some cases for over a year, for ten services I no longer used.

Incredibly wasteful, but I'm hardly alone. This week, I learned the average millennial has seventeen subscriptions.[156] And most of us, millennials or not, have too many we no longer need. It's never been easier to accumulate unused subscriptions. To sign up and forget while ignoring the charges on your credit card or the inbox full of unread newsletters.

We're oversubscribed.

Not just in our inboxes and on our credit cards but everywhere else. The act of signing up for something or someone extends beyond the digital checkout page. We're oversubscribed to people, ideas, and projects. We accumulate clutter and waste in every part of our lives. We keep subscribing but rarely opt-out.

In 1957, writer E. B. White recounted his trouble getting rid of things he had accumulated in his apartment in New York. While he was writing about physical clutter in his home, we face the same challenge in getting rid of subscriptions in our lives:

> A home is like a reservoir equipped with a check valve: the valve permits influx but prevents outflow. Acquisition goes on night and day—smoothly, subtly, imperceptibly. I have no sharp taste for acquiring things, but it is not necessary to desire things in order to acquire them.[157]

Our lives have the same imbalance of inflow and outflow. The modern problem of digital subscriptions is just a new way to accumulate what we no longer desire. But they're not the only subscriptions we need to examine.

As you pursue your defiant goals, you'll encounter distractions everywhere. By limiting your goals, choices, and efforts, you prevent self-inflicted distractions in the future. But you're not starting from a blank page. One result of conformity is a life cluttered with ideas, people, and projects that aren't aligned with where you're headed.

Goals that challenge the status quo demand the best of you, because they are rooted in something deeper: your manifesto. It's a vision for who you want to be, not just what you want to achieve. Now comes the harder part: protecting that vision.

Go check your credit card and review your inbox, but don't stop there. To master conformity and become rationally defiant, you need to let go of the subscriptions to the status quo that weigh you down.

REVIEW RELATIONSHIPS

The longest-running study on adult development—Harvard's eighty-year research project—found that the single strongest predictor of long-term well-being wasn't wealth, intelligence, or career success. It was the quality of your relationships.[158]

The wrong relationships don't just distract you; they derail you. This is true not only of friendships or romantic partners but also of collaborators, business partners, and mentors. The people you surround yourself with shape your habits, beliefs, and emotional energy. They reinforce who you are, or who you were.

When you're pursuing bold, defiant goals, you need the right people around you. If you're serious about your manifesto and the goals you've committed to, you need to be serious about who comes with you.

Start with this question: if I met this person today, would I choose to spend time with them, knowing who I'm becoming?

It's a confronting question because it reminds you that your current commitment to someone is an ongoing choice. Every relationship is a subscription: a commitment of time, energy, and identity. Too many of us keep paying for connections that no longer serve the life we're trying to build.

But here's the problem: most of us don't even realize we're choosing. We stay in relationships by default, because of history, habit, or fear, until you realize they're pulling you down. Lowering your ambition. Reinforcing doubt.

Dan Sullivan stated his version of this idea like this: "Surround yourself with people who remind you more of your future than your past."[159]

That's the test. Does this relationship reflect your future or your history? Does it support your defiant goals or distract you from them?

Answering honestly is easiest for people we're the least committed to. We've all had friendships we've outgrown. Sometimes it's us, and sometimes it's them. But we know when the connection is lost. It's not hard to let go of people on the edges of our circles.

It's harder to be objective about the people closest to us. Close friends, romantic partners, and family members are in a different emotional category from the come-and-go friendships we accept as transient. We've invested more time, energy, and emotion into these relationships, and so have they. Yet these are exactly the connections that are the most important for our new path. They're the ones who make achieving difficult, defiant goals easier, or impossible.

That doesn't mean every challenge to your vision is a threat. Don't surround yourself with yes-people. Great relationships stretch us, push us, and hold up honest mirrors. But they don't cheer for your failure. And they don't require you to shrink to stay connected.

The best relationships have ups and downs. All partners disagree occasionally, and sometimes, we're expected to give more than we receive. There's no objective accounting in relationships. But learn to see a temporary wobble over a genuine sign it's time to move on. Would you invest in this relationship if you met them today? If the answer is no, the right move may be to let go.

Until you clear the space, there's no room for the people who truly believe in what you're creating and who you're becoming. Your relationships are either ladders or anchors. Choose accordingly.

CANCEL OLD BELIEFS

When I think of David Goggins, I picture a Navy SEAL, an ultra-endurance athlete, and a symbol of relentless mental toughness. Which is even more remarkable considering where he started from. But in reading his story, it's clear his transformation wasn't measured in miles but in mindset.

Goggins grew up in an abusive household, struggled in school, and was told he had a learning disability. By his early twenties, he was overweight, depressed, and working as a night-shift exterminator, numbing himself with milkshakes and self-doubt. Reflecting on that time, he wrote, "Denial is the ultimate comfort zone."[160]

Everything changed the day he saw a documentary about Navy SEALs. He saw what he wasn't and decided to become it. He gave himself ninety days to lose over one hundred pounds and meet the entrance requirements. But it didn't start with push-ups or running.

It started with belief. "The most important conversations you'll ever have are the ones you'll have with yourself," he later wrote. "You have to be willing to go to war with yourself and create a whole new identity."[161]

Goggins didn't just train harder. He stopped believing he wasn't able to achieve greatness. He rewired his identity. He defied his personal status quo, and everything changed.

This is the power and the danger of beliefs. They shape not just what we think but what we attempt. Goggins's story is extreme, but the pattern is universal: we all carry beliefs that define our limits long before we test them.

Psychologist Carol Dweck's research on mindset reveals how this works. People with a "fixed mindset" believe their abilities are static—you're either smart or you're not, talented or you're not. Those with a "growth mindset" believe abilities can be developed. The difference? Fixed-mindset individuals avoid challenges that might reveal inadequacy. Growth-mindset individuals see challenges as opportunities to improve. Same situation, different belief, completely different life trajectory.[162]

These limiting beliefs are particularly dangerous because they're often invisible. They're not conscious thoughts but background assumptions. They are mental subscriptions that were installed years ago by parents, teachers, communities, or past versions of ourselves. We never paused to examine them. Now we're paying the price in ways we don't even recognize.

To move forward, you have to surface these buried beliefs. Here's how.

Start by auditing your beliefs. Write down what you believe about yourself, your capabilities, your work, and your future. Don't filter. Include the ugly ones: "I'm not creative." "I don't deserve success." "People like me don't do things like that."

Once you have them visible, use a technique called laddering to identify the core belief underlying them. Here's how it works for someone pursuing a defiant career change:

Surface belief: "I can't leave my corporate job to start a business."

Why do I believe that?

"Because I need the steady income."

Why do I need steady income more than opportunity?

"Because financial instability terrifies me."

Why does it terrify me?

"Because I grew up watching my parents struggle with money."

Why does that mean I'll struggle?

"Because I learned that financial risk leads to suffering."

Core belief revealed: "Taking risks with money always leads to pain."

Now you have something real to examine. Is this belief actually true? Does financial risk *always* lead to suffering, or did you inherit a fear from people operating in different circumstances with different capabilities?

The revelation often comes when you realize the belief isn't yours. It's a hand-me-down fear from someone else's experience. A "truth" absorbed before you could evaluate it. A limitation you accepted before you could test it.

The process of changing beliefs isn't comfortable. Cognitive dissonance, the discomfort of holding conflicting beliefs, makes us want to retreat to familiar thoughts. That's why most people would rather defend a limiting belief than examine it.

Here's what Goggins understood: the pain of changing your beliefs is temporary. The pain of being imprisoned by them is permanent.

Start with one belief that's holding you back from your defiant goals. Put it through the ladder. Trace it to its source. Ask: Is this actually true? Is it helpful? Did I choose it, or did I inherit it?

Then rewrite it. Not with empty affirmations but with something you can actually believe. Instead of "Taking risks with money always leads to pain," try "I can learn to take calculated risks." Instead of "People like me don't succeed," try "I define my own potential."

These aren't magic words. They're permission slips. Permission to attempt what your old beliefs made impossible. You can't pursue defiant goals while subscribed to conformist beliefs. One has to go.

OPT-OUT OF FAKE DEMANDS

In 1845, Henry David Thoreau built a one-room cabin on the edge of Walden Pond and lived there for two years, two months, and two days. He grew beans, took long walks, and wrote. But more than anything, he was there to reflect and figure out what truly mattered before stepping into the rest of his life. As he later wrote:

> I went to the woods because I wished to live deliberately, to front only the essential facts of life, and see if I could not learn what it had to teach, and not, when I came to die, discover that I had not lived.[163]

More than a century later, in 1975, a broke and unknown actor named Sylvester Stallone watched the underdog boxer, Chuck Wepner, go fifteen rounds with Muhammad Ali. Inspired, he went home and wrote the first draft of *Rocky* in just over three days. To make it happen, he painted his apartment windows black, blocking out light, distraction, and everything else that wasn't the story he was determined to write.

Most of us aren't escaping to the woods or blacking out our homes. But these extreme examples reveal something important: sometimes, the only way to make space for what matters is to eliminate what doesn't.

Work, side projects, hobbies, family time, errands—our list of commitments is endless. How we fill our time either energizes us or quietly drains us. And often, the things that used to feel meaningful become misaligned with who we're becoming. This is one of the most overlooked sources of distraction from your defiant goals: you're still committed to things that no longer fit your future.

Ask yourself: if I designed my ideal life today, would this commitment make the list?

Most of us don't feel like we're choosing our commitments at all. We're reacting, rushing, and fulfilling expectations we've never stopped to evaluate.

Of course, some commitments are actual obligations: caring for your children or aging parents, paying your bills, and showing up for a partner. These are the nonnegotiables. Defying them isn't bold; it's selfish.

Beyond that, things get blurry. You might be clinging to work projects you never wanted in the first place. Still leading groups or committees you said yes to five years ago. Still hosting that monthly get-together out of guilt or routine. Still chasing a goal that hasn't excited you in years.

These aren't obligations. They're choices you forgot were choices. And just like relationships and beliefs, you can outgrow them.

A helpful place to start is with a time audit. Notice where your time goes each day, how your weeks get filled, and what consistently occupies your seasons and years. Then distinguish between the obligations you truly must uphold and the activities you've carried forward without questioning. For each one, ask: does this support the future I've committed to? Or does it reflect a version of myself I've already outgrown?

This process reveals two things. First, we often have more control over our time than we think. Life feels like an endless sprint between duties, but when we pause and look closely, much of our busyness is optional. Second, many things filling our calendar—our evenings, energy, and bandwidth—aren't aligned with who we're becoming. Some never were. When that's the case, they slow us down.

This is why the earlier stages of Rational Defiance, setting your manifesto and goals, matter so much. Once you know where you want to go, it becomes easier to see what doesn't belong on the path.

Letting go of outdated commitments isn't about doing less. It's about making room for what matters more. It's about creating a life that's aligned, not just busy.

SUBSCRIBE WITH CAUTION

Marie Kondo became famous for helping people clean their closets. But what made her work stick were simple principles, such as "Keep only those things that speak to your heart. Discard the rest."

The same logic applies to your time, beliefs, and commitments. Keep only what speaks to your future. Every subscription, whether to a person, an idea, or a project, comes at a cost. Not just in money but in attention, energy, and mental bandwidth. If it's not aligned, it's noise.

Derek Sivers offers a wonderfully simple rule: "If you're not saying 'HELL YEAH!' about something, say 'no.'"[164] That's your filter now. For new ideas, for new relationships, for new opportunities; unless they clearly support your manifesto and your defiant goals, let them go.

And keep letting them go. A year after I first reviewed my subscriptions (the digital ones I opened this chapter with), I reviewed them again. Despite everything I'd learned, I'd collected more. More apps. More tools. More memberships. And once again, I had to clean up.

Unsubscribing isn't a onetime purge. It's a mindset. A discipline. Decluttering your life is how you make space for what matters most. But keeping it that way? That's how you stay free.

You've set your course. You've cleared the distractions. What matters now is whether you can stay the course when conformity fights back—and it always does.

CHAPTER TWELVE

Stay Defiant

IN A FAMOUS TALE IN GREEK MYTHOLOGY, ZEUS, THE KING of the gods, forbade mortals from having fire. Prometheus defied the gods by stealing fire and giving it to humanity. His act unlocked our ability to cook, forge, and create civilization. For his rebellion, the punishment was brutal.

Zeus had him chained to a rock, where each day, an eagle devoured his liver, only for it to regenerate overnight and be eaten again. Over and over.

None of us fears such a mythical backlash for stepping out of line. But the fear of consequences for defiance is real. The moment you choose to live differently, speak up, or pursue something unconventional, the doubts rush in.

What if they reject me? What if I'm wrong? What if I lose what I have?

Most people don't abandon their plans because the ideas are bad. They abandon them because the fear shows up before the resistance does. And that fear is often misplaced. As Seneca wrote, "We suffer more in imagination than in reality."[165]

We worry about what others will think when most people

aren't thinking about us at all. We wonder whether we have what it takes instead of finding out. We wait until the world is ready instead of showing it why it should be.

That doesn't mean there won't be obstacles. Some resistance is real, and it's coming. Not everyone will understand your path. Not every system will welcome change. You'll face pushback from old habits, from peers who feel threatened, and from environments designed to reward predictability more than progress.

This chapter is about what happens next. You've written your manifesto. You've set your defiant goals. You've cleared the distractions. And what you do from here, how you respond to fear and friction, will determine whether your defiance stays a thought or becomes something real.

If you've come this far, it's time to hold your defiant resolve.

PREPARE FOR RESISTANCE

Resistance arrives in many forms. Outright rejection and disapproval are the most obvious. But often, it shows up as polite hesitation. Quiet skepticism. Reasonable-sounding doubts. They're just as likely to show up in your own head as they are in others' reactions.

If you're doing something defiant, objections are not a surprise. They are part of the process. Your aim is not to avoid them but to prepare for them. One of my favorite examples is from, of all places, a controversial 1956 poem.

Allen Ginsberg's *Howl* was filled with images of sex, drugs, jazz, madness, and protest, written amidst the conformity of 1950s America. At a time when the culture demanded silence, order, and moral restraint, *Howl* was loud, chaotic, obscene, and utterly defiant.

Everyone knew it would cause trouble. Lawrence Ferlinghetti, founder of City Lights Books, planned to publish it. But instead of waiting for the trouble to arrive, he prepared for it.[166]

Before the book even went to press, he contacted the American Civil Liberties Union (ACLU) and asked them to defend it when the inevitable obscenity charges came. They agreed. And when the police seized copies, and Ferlinghetti was arrested, the defense was already in motion. Literary critics testified. The ACLU argued the case. Ultimately, the court ruled that the poem had redeeming artistic value. It became a landmark free-speech case because Ferlinghetti had anticipated the objections and prepared his response.

That's what it means to think like a defiant strategist. Not just to shoot your shot but to know what's coming back. Of course, most defiance doesn't end in arrest or court cases. Your resistance might be a skeptical boss, confused family members, or your own self-doubt at 3:00 a.m. But the principle remains: if you're doing anything defiantly, whether starting something unconventional, challenging a norm, or changing how things are done, you'll face objections. Preparation is what will make you successful when it happens.

Good salespeople understand this. They call it "objection handling," the discipline of anticipating pushback before it happens. They don't get rattled when someone says, "We're not ready" or "We're already using a competitor." They expect it. They've prepared their responses. That readiness turns resistance into conversation.

The same principle applies when you challenge the status quo. You are selling a new idea to people who are still subscribed to the old one.

Go back to the idea you're pursuing, whether it's a bold change at work, a new business model, or a reinvention of how you live, and build your objection list.

If you want to implement a radically new way of working in your company, consider where you'll meet resistance.

Start with your own doubts. What hesitations are already circling in your head?

Objection: What if I'm not the kind of person who can pull this off?

Response: You become that person by trying. No one feels ready at first. Action shapes identity. Courage comes from doing, not waiting.

Then, move outward. What will others push back on?

Objection: This isn't how we do things.

Response: Show what's possible. Share precedents. Offer a safe trial or limited rollout.

And finally, consider the constraints of your environment.

Objection: Our tools or systems won't support this.

Response: Prepare alternatives. Show how others have adapted. Highlight the cost of not changing.

This strategy doesn't just apply to work. Whether you're starting a movement or making a personal shift others don't understand, anticipating resistance and preparing your response gives your defiance a chance to take root. You don't have to win every argument. But you do have to walk into the resistance prepared. Anticipating objections makes your idea more likely to survive.

You are not just the visionary. You are the strategist. Resistance is part of the game. Write your list. Practice your replies. Then, keep going.

FIND YOUR ALLIES

Your defiance might start alone, but you can't go far that way. While preparation helps you face resistance, allies help you overcome it.

An earlier chapter showed why you should let go of relationships that no longer serve your direction. To make space. This is where you fill it with the right people. Defiance is a personal vision that becomes possible when shared. I know this firsthand.

When I set out to build a digital research agency, I didn't do it alone. I partnered with Elna, a fellow intern fresh out of university, and from the beginning, we shared a defiant vision: to build the leading digital research agency on the continent. At the time, the research industry still relied heavily on face-to-face interviews, focus groups, and call centers.

We were twenty-four with barely a year of experience, offering a fully digital alternative—in an industry that associates new with unproven and unreliable. To most, we were too young, too new, and too different to take seriously. It made for a less-than-spectacular first few months in business. But having each other as allies in the cause made it easier to persist.

Slowly, but steadily, other allies emerged. Six months in, a financial services company gave us a chance. It started as a pilot. It became our biggest client for years. That success helped us win over the next one, and the next. One client became ten. Ten became fifty. And slowly, the agency grew to serve hundreds of clients.

On the inside, a few early believers joined the team, which grew to over sixty people a decade later.

None of that would have happened without early allies on the inside and the outside.

Here's what those years taught me about finding and recognizing allies:

- **They don't always announce themselves:** Allies aren't louder than your critics. They're the ones who linger after the meeting to ask a question. The ones who forward your idea to someone they know. The ones who say, "I'm not sure, but this is interesting."
- **Look for curiosity over certainty:** The person who says "tell me more" is often more valuable than the one who immediately agrees. Questions mean engagement. Hesitation that turns into consideration often becomes your strongest support.
- **Not all allies look the same:** Some share your vision and want to help build it with you. Some cheer you on from the sidelines. Others bring credibility, access, or influence. Don't expect one perfect ally. Look for people who bring the piece you're missing.
- **Be patient:** In our case, that financial services company wasn't ready to be our ally on day one. But six months later, something had shifted. Stay in contact with potential allies even when they're not ready yet.

Whether you're launching something new, challenging the rules, or simply choosing a different path, finding the right people early changes everything. As you deal with the criticism and resistance, learn to spot the subtle nods of agreement from those who are coming around to your vision. They may be few, but even one ally doubles the force of your effort.

Don't wait for the crowd. Find your first allies. Then watch your vision multiply.

BUILD YOUR IDENTITY

Assembling the pieces—manifesto in hand, goals mapped out, distractions cleared, objections expected, allies at your side—shapes something deeper. The internal transformation is the true measure of how far you've come. At a certain point, defiance stops being something you do and becomes who you are.

I mean this in two ways. Achieving your defiant ambitions is the most visible of these changes.

In the early 1930s, blues guitarist Robert Johnson was known only for being forgettable. Playing alongside legends like Son House and Willie Brown, no one paid attention. His playing was stiff; his voice thin. Most dismissed him entirely.

Then he disappeared.

When Johnson returned after months away, something had changed. His technique was spellbinding. His playing was fluid, haunting, and entirely his own. People who had dismissed him were stunned.

Rumors spread that he sold his soul to the devil at a crossroads for his newfound gift. The truth was simpler and harder: he had gone away to practice, to struggle, and to remake himself. He returned not just improved but transformed into an artist who would reshape American music.

This is one outcome: achieving the defiant goal you set for yourself. Johnson wanted to become a master musician in a world that had already dismissed him. He achieved his ambition through transformation.

This visible achievement happens everywhere. The overweight person who defies their history to become an athlete. The immigrant who arrives with nothing and builds an empire. The addict who gets clean and becomes a counselor. The stutterer who becomes an orator. The abuse survivor who becomes an advocate. Each individual began with a defiant ambition—to become something the world said they couldn't be—and made it a reality through transformation. These are the before-and-after photos of defiance.

But there's another kind of transformation. Becoming a more defiant version of yourself. Not just achieving something different but becoming someone who lives defiance as a daily practice.

Andrei Sakharov was the Soviet Union's star physicist, designer of the hydrogen bomb, and decorated hero of the state. The model of conformity. But while watching the arms race and suppression of intellectual freedom, something shifted.

In 1968, he published *Reflections on Progress, Peaceful Coexistence, and Intellectual Freedom*, openly criticizing the Soviet system. He didn't just change his mind—he became an open dissident of the regime he formerly supported.

The transformation came at a price. Over the following years, the state gradually stripped his privileges and honors. By 1980, they exiled him internally to Gorky. Throughout the 1970s and 1980s, he faced escalating harassment. But he kept writing, speaking, and pushing. Each act of defiance deepened his transformation. He became someone who couldn't stop telling the truth, regardless of the cost.

This deeper transformation is evident in everyday examples too. The employee who speaks up in meetings after years of silence. The parent who stops living through their children and pursues their own dreams. The artist who stops creating for galleries and starts creating what they believe in. The executive who walks away from prestige to build something meaningful. They haven't just achieved a goal; they've become people who can't help but challenge what doesn't serve them.

Johnson achieved his defiant ambition: mastery despite dismissal. Sakharov became a defiant person: someone fundamentally unable to accept lies. Both transformations matter. One changes what you can do. The other changes who you are.

Becoming defiant is rarely a single decision. It's a slow crossing from who you've been to who your vision requires. In that space, there's doubt, friction, and fear. But also clarity. Every boundary questioned, every risk faced, pulls you deeper into alignment with your future self.

You become the person who speaks up when it's easier to stay quiet. The one who does what's right even when it's unpopular. Who values integrity more than approval. Who chooses their future over their past. Who creates instead of conforms. Who lives by belief, not by default. Who walks away from the safe path when it stops leading anywhere worth going.

If you're not there yet, remember Rick Rubin's words, "You're not who you were. You're not who you will be. You're in the in-between."[167]

The in-between is where the work happens. Where manifestos and goals are created, subscriptions canceled, and resistance anticipated. Stay in that space long enough, with enough intention, and one day you'll realize you're no longer trying to be defiant. You simply are.

KEEP GOING

There is no magic formula that eradicates resistance from your journey. Despite your best efforts, sometimes you'll fail. Just make sure you fail on the field, by showing up and not staying on the sidelines out of the fear that comes in many forms: embarrassment, uncertainty, rejection, or failure...The list is long.

Some fear is protective. You probably shouldn't invest all your savings into a startup that makes edible shoelaces. Fortune doesn't always favor the brave. It's a reminder to prepare, to check your assumptions, and to think critically.

Many fears are irrational. There's a gap between feelings and facts. When we needlessly conform, we remain safe and comfortable, but we lose out on so much more: speaking the truth, starting a movement, pursuing the dream job, discovering our passions...This list is even longer. Because most fear is restrictive. It prevents the attempt, not the failure. It doesn't come from truth. It comes from old stories, imagined judgments, and inherited scripts.

Your job is to separate the two. One keeps you safe. The other keeps you stuck. In a 2014 commencement speech at the Maharishi University, Jim Carrey shared this lesson:

> Fear is going to be a player in your life, but you get to decide how much. You can spend your whole life imagining ghosts, worrying about the pathway to the future, but all there will ever be is what's happening here, and the decisions we make in this moment, which are based in either love or fear. So many of us choose our path out of fear disguised as practicality. What we really want seems impossibly out of reach and ridiculous to expect. So we never dare to ask the universe for it. I'm saying I'm the proof that you can ask the universe for it. Please. And if it doesn't happen for you right away, it's only because the universe is so busy fulfilling my order. Party size.
>
> My father could have been a great comedian, but he didn't believe that was possible for him. And so he made a conservative choice. Instead, he got a safe job as an accountant. And when I was 12 years old, he was let go from that safe job and our family had to do whatever we could to survive. I learned many great lessons from my father, not the least of which was that you can fail at

what you don't want so you might as well take a chance on doing what you love.[168]

The hard truth is this: Most people don't fail because they tried and lost. They fail because they never try. Jerry Seinfeld, another comedian, shared a piece of advice he once got from David Letterman, "Make sure you fail doing exactly what you want to do...That you can live with."[169]

Failure on your own terms is hard, but failure while conforming is worse.

Your resolve doesn't come from the ignorant consistency of conformity. It comes from seeing the world clearly, taking a stand for what you want and what the world needs, and pursuing it despite the obstacles you'll face.

You don't have to eliminate fear. You just have to act anyway. To keep moving even when no one claps. To keep building when the outcome is uncertain. To stay defiant, even when you're the only one left standing.

So choose: your fear or your future.

Conclusion

Your Turn

IN 1967, KATHRINE SWITZER DID SOMETHING BOTH SIMPLE and revolutionary: she ran the Boston Marathon.

For seventy years, the race had been men-only. It wasn't just tradition. Boston Athletic Association (BAA) director Will Cloney stated plainly that women were physically incapable of running twenty-six miles.

But twenty-year-old Switzer had been running ten miles every night with her coach, Arnie Briggs. When she mentioned wanting to run Boston, even Briggs initially protested, "No woman can run the Boston Marathon." She reminded him that Bobbi Gibb had jumped in unofficially the year before and finished. They made a deal: if she could run the marathon distance in practice, he'd take her to Boston.

She did. And when race day came, she registered as "K. V. Switzer," received her official number, and started running.

For the first few miles, everything seemed fine. She ran alongside Briggs and her boyfriend, Tom Miller, her hooded sweatshirt concealing her identity. Then the hood slipped off. That's when race co-director Jock Semple saw her.

Semple, a traditionalist known for chasing off anyone he deemed unserious about his race, exploded. He jumped from the press truck and charged after her, screaming, "Get the hell out of my race and give me those numbers!" In her memoir, Switzer recalls: "Instinctively I jerked my head around quickly and looked square into the most vicious face I'd ever seen. A big man, a huge man, with bared teeth was set to pounce, and before I could react he grabbed my shoulder and flung me back."[170]

The famous photograph captures what happened next: Semple trying to rip off her numbers, Briggs getting knocked to the ground defending her, Miller body-checking Semple away. In the chaos, Switzer lost a glove but kept her numbers. And kept running.

> I knew if I quit, nobody would ever believe that women had the capability to run the marathon distance. If I quit, everybody would say it was a publicity stunt. If I quit, it would set women's sports back, way back, instead of forward. If I quit, I'd never run Boston. If I quit, Jock Semple and all those like him would win. My fear and humiliation turned to anger.[171]

She finished in 4:20. But the BAA's response was telling. With women's supposed inability now disproven, director Cloney shifted arguments:

> Women can't run in the marathon because the rules forbid it. Unless we have rules, society will be in chaos. I don't make the rules, but I try to carry them out. We have no place in the marathon for any unauthorized person, even a man. If that girl were my daughter, I would spank her.[172]

Initially, officials doubled down. The Amateur Athletic Union banned women from all competitions with male runners. It took five years before Boston officially accepted women in 1972.

But Switzer didn't wait for permission. She kept running, kept pushing. In 1977, she created the Avon International Running Circuit, a worldwide series that helped establish women's marathon running globally and paved the way for the Olympic women's marathon in 1984. Switzer was named female runner of the decade (1967–1977) by *Runner's World* magazine and later became an Emmy award-winning television commentator for marathons.

The photograph of Semple attacking her became iconic, a visual reminder of what happens when you defy senseless rules.[173] At every Boston Marathon since, women runners approach her with tears in their eyes. "They're weeping for joy," she says, "because running has changed their lives. They feel they can do anything."[174]

Semple's story also matters here. The man immortalized as the face of backward thinking? He changed. "Once the rule was adjusted and women were allowed in the race," race organizer Marja Bakker explained, "Jock was one of their staunchest supporters." He and Switzer became friends. Semple died of cancer in 1988, and until the end, Switzer would visit him at the hospital where he was being treated.

* * *

This story is a microcosm of the ideas in this book.

The running community and society-at-large were deeply stuck in a Conformity Coma. So unconsciously attached to "how things are done," they couldn't see the absurdity of banning half the population from running. It reveals all the signs of the conformity traps in Part I of this book.

The race organizers' reactions stemmed from a need to remain *consistent* with their prior positions. Jock Semple had a history of removing what he considered unserious runners, and he considered Switzer another example of this trend. BAA director Will Cloney didn't update his thinking but just shifted his argument from biology to bureaucracy. "Unless we have rules, society will be in chaos." Classic cognitive dissonance: when facts threaten beliefs, double down on the beliefs.

There's also the role of *compliance*. Cloney admitted he had no part in creating these rules, but he followed them to avoid the descent into chaos that would ensue if he didn't. Semple was also just following the rules, which he understood to be that no woman was allowed to enter the marathon. Rules are a powerful example of formalized social influence. And, as we have seen, even when the rules don't make sense, people tend to comply.

For seventy years, everyone accepted that women couldn't run marathons. Their *complacency* blinded many people to the irrationality of this attitude. Even Switzer's coach initially parroted the accepted wisdom, "No woman can run the Boston Marathon."

This is obviously also a story about Rational Defiance, from Part II of the book. Switzer's 1967 Boston Marathon defied the status quo, leading to a remarkable positive impact on her own life and many others. She didn't rebel aimlessly. She saw that something better was possible, chose this specific battle, acted deliberately, and was willing to stand apart. She continued her defiance in the years that followed, championing the cause she stood for. Her mindset showed the foundational skills that enabled her defiance.

She *saw clearly* what others didn't. Switzer answered her

coach's critical reaction to her marathon aspirations, "Why not? I run ten miles every night?" She reminded him that Bobbi Gibb had jumped into the race, unofficially, the previous year and completed it. She, and other pioneers like Gibb, saw what was obvious all along: not allowing women to run marathons is completely irrational. Her skepticism of the status quo propelled her belief that it was worth challenging.

She was willing to *seek radical ideas and experiment*. There were no women's running teams at Syracuse University, where Switzer was a nineteen-year-old journalism student. So she joined the men's cross-country team. It was where she met her coach, Arnie Briggs, who had run fifteen Boston Marathons. Their evening sessions consisted of Arnie telling her stories of the Marathon to get her through the sessions. Switzer recalls she "loved listening to them—until this night when I snapped and said, 'Oh Arnie, let's quit *talking* about the Boston Marathon and run the damn thing!'"[175] That's when the deal was made to attempt the marathon distance in training. Her exposure to these inputs and ideas expanded her perception of what was possible. And her willingness to plan a test of her abilities laid the foundation for her plans.

Pursuing her defiant Direction, the focus of Part III of the book, came next.

Switzer was led by a strong set of convictions. Her actions reveal someone who *stood for something*. She wasn't content with sitting on the sidelines. She once remarked, "Life is for participating, not spectating."[176] Her contentious participation in 1967 was followed by a life dedicated to enabling female athletes to participate rather than spectate.

Once she knew her destination, she *set her course*, complete with goals and a plan. And the goal she set was uniquely hers: to do what no woman runner had done before. With her participation in the Boston Marathon settled after her successful trial with her coach, she remembers: "'Hot damn,' I thought, 'I have a coach, a partner, a plan, and a goal—the biggest race in the world. Boston! *Boston!*'"[177]

Switzer *overcame distractions* and obstacles, *maintaining her defiant resolve*. She wasn't stopped by an initially skeptical coach or rules that prevented her from participating. She kept running despite the physical resistance from Jock Semple and kept pushing the cause of women's running forward in the decades after the race. She found her allies—the support from her dad, her boyfriend, and coach. Millions of male and female allies joined the cause in the years after. Most importantly, she held her resolve when it mattered most: "My fear and humiliation turned to anger." She used the very emotion meant to stop her as fuel to continue. Her story shows both types of defiant transformation. She achieved her defiant ambition: finishing the marathon when the world said women couldn't. But more importantly, she became someone who couldn't stop fighting for what she believed in and dedicated her life to opening doors for others.

Even Semple's eventual transformation proves a deeper point: today's fierce defenders of the status quo might be tomorrow's supporters, once the new reality becomes undeniable. The Conformity Coma can break, even in its strongest supporters.

TIME TO SWIM

Switzer's story shows what's possible when one person stops floating and starts swimming. But here's what matters more: she wasn't superhuman. She was a twenty-year-old college student who enjoyed running. She didn't have special training in activism or social change. She just saw something that didn't make sense and took action.

Rational Defiance doesn't require extraordinary courage or unusual talent. It requires seeing clearly enough to spot the absurdity, caring enough to act, and persisting when they try to pull you off course.

This book began with Hunter S. Thompson's question: whether to float with the tide or swim for a goal. By now, you understand how deep the current runs. You've seen how conformity operates through consistency, compliance, and complacency. You've learned to see clearly, seek radical inputs, and experiment with unconventional paths. You know how to stand for something, set your course, clear distractions, and hold your resolve.

The question now isn't whether you understand these ideas. It's whether you'll use them.

Because somewhere in your life, there's a marathon you're not supposed to run. A rule that makes no sense. A limitation that exists only because everyone believes it. Maybe it's the career path you're told is unrealistic. The creative work you're told won't sell. The lifestyle that doesn't fit the template. The truth you know but won't say.

You know what it is. You've thought about it while reading this book. You've imagined what would happen if you actually did it. You've probably already listed all the reasons why you can't, why now isn't the right time, and why you should wait until conditions are perfect.

But conditions are never perfect. There's never a right time. There's only the choice you make right now: to keep floating or start swimming.

Here's what I know: The regret of trying and failing fades. The regret of never trying only grows. Every day you delay is another day living someone else's life. Another day accepting rules that make no sense. Another day choosing comfort over courage.

You don't need to attack a global injustice or start a movement. Start with one area where you've been floating. Apply what you've learned. Question the assumption everyone accepts. Try the experiment everyone says won't work. Speak the truth everyone pretends not to know.

Start small if you need to, but start. Because Rational Defiance isn't a philosophy you agree with—it's a practice you live. Every time you choose your path over the prescribed one, you prove something important: the status quo is optional. Conformity is a choice. We can create rules that make more sense than the ones we inherited.

Switzer didn't just win the right for women to run marathons. She demonstrated that when you refuse to accept senseless limitations, you expand what is possible for everyone. The same goes for all the famous and unknown deviants in this book and out there in the world. Your defiance might not make headlines, but it matters. To you, certainly. But also to everyone who sees you choose courage over compliance.

So here's my challenge: Before you close this book, write down one thing—just one—where you've been conforming against your better judgment. Then do something about it today. Not tomorrow. Not when you feel ready. Today.

Send the email. Have the conversation. Start the project. Say no to the obligation. Say yes to the possibility. Take one action that moves you from floating to swimming.

This is your life. Your only life. You can spend it floating toward a destination you never wanted. Or you can decide what matters to you and swim for it. Deliberately. Defiantly. Starting now.

The tide is strong. It always will be. It's time you learn to swim.

Notes

1 Hunter S. Thompson, *The Proud Highway: Saga of a Desperate Southern Gentleman, 1955–1967* (Ballantine Books, 1997), 117.

2 Thompson, *Proud Highway*, 119.

3 Steve Stewart-Williams, *The Ape That Understood the Universe: How the Mind and Culture Evolve* (Cambridge University Press, 2018), 240.

4 Carlin, George. "The 11 O'Clock News." *FM & AM*. Little David Records LD 7214, 1972, LP; Carlin, George. *Brain Droppings* (Hyperion, 1997), 164.

5 Bonnie Ware, "Regrets of the Dying," *Bonnie Ware* (blog), accessed October 4, 2025, https://bronnieware.com/blog/regrets-of-the-dying/.

6 Dan Sullivan and Benjamin Hardy, *Who Not How: The Formula to Achieve Bigger Goals Through Accelerating Teamwork* (Hay House, 2020), 24.

7 Chris Maume, "Gail Zappa: Frank Zappa's Wife, Muse and Manager Who Ferociously Protected His Musical Legacy," *The Independent*, October 12, 2015, https://www.the-independent.com/news/obituaries/gail-zappa-frank-zappa-s-wife-muse-and-manager-who-ferociously-protected-his-musical-legacy-a6691251.html.

8 Frank Zappa, "Frank Zappa on Guitar Solos, Improvisation, and Spontaneity," interview by Nina Blackwell, video televised on MTV, December 8, 1984, posted January 17, 2016, by Paul Dezelski, YouTube, 00:03:44, https://www.youtube.com/watch?v=A6ZzTr-a2L8.

9 Robert Nozick, *Anarchy, State, and Utopia* (Basic Books, 1974), 42–45.

10 Felipe De Brigard, "If You Like It, Does It Matter If It's Real?," *Philosophical Psychology* 23, no. 1 (2010): 47, https://doi.org/10.1080/09515080903532290.

11 De Brigard, "If You Like It," 47.

12 De Brigard, "If You Like It," 47–48.

13 William Samuelson and Richard Zeckhauser, "Status Quo Bias in Decision Making," *Journal of Risk and Uncertainty* 1, no. 1 (1988): 7–59, https://doi.org/10.1007/BF00055564.

14 Samuelson and Zeckhauser, "Status Quo Bias," 12–13.

15 Samuelson and Zeckhauser, "Status Quo Bias," 12.

16 Samuelson and Zeckhauser, "Status Quo Bias," 12–13.

17 Samuelson and Zeckhauser, "Status Quo Bias," 14–19.

18 Eric J. Johnson and Daniel Goldstein, "Do Defaults Save Lives?," *Science* 302, no. 5649 (2003): 1338, https://doi.org/10.1126/science.1091721.

19 Ben Wigert and Ryan Pendell, "7 Workplace Challenges for 2025," Gallup, December 15, 2024, https://www.gallup.com/workplace/654329/workplace-challenges-2025.aspx.

20 Henry D. Thoreau, *Walden; Or, Life in the Woods* (Ticknor and Fields, 1854), 29.

21 Angela Duckworth, forward to *How to Change: The Science of Getting from Where You Are to Where You Want to Be*, by Katy Milkman (Portfolio/Penguin, 2021), xiii.

22 John Steinbeck, *Travels with Charley: In Search of America* (Penguin Books, 2002), 64.

23 Nathaniel Branden, *The Six Pillars of Self-Esteem* (Bantam, 1994), 67–68.

24 Blaise Pascal, *Pensées*, trans. W. F. Trotter (Dover Publications, 2003), 28–29.

25 William James, *The Principles of Psychology: Vol. I* (Henry Holt and Company, 1910), 104.

26 Stobaeus, *Anthology* III.17.10, cited in Gabriele Giannantoni, *Socratis et Socraticorum Reliquiae*, vol. 5 (Naples: Bibliopolis, 1990), V B 75.

27 Jean-Jacques Rousseau, *The Social Contract and Discourses*, trans. G. D. H. Cole, rev. J. H. Brumfitt and John C. Hall (J. M. Dent & Sons, 1973), 181.

28 Oscar Wilde, *De Profundis* (G. P. Putnam's Sons, 1905), 63.

29 Niccolò Machiavelli, *The Prince*, trans. Luigi Ricci, rev. E. R. P. Vincent (Oxford University Press, 1939), 24.

30 Ralph Waldo Emerson, *The Journals of Ralph Waldo Emerson*, ed. Robert N. Linscott (Random House, 1960), 218.

31 Kemp, Simon. "Digital 2024: Global Overview Report." DataReportal, January 31, 2024. https://datareportal.com/reports/digital-2024-global-overview-report.

32 Dorothy L. Sayers, *The Lost Tools of Learning* (Methuen & Co., 1948), 12.

33 William James, *Talks to Teachers on Psychology: And to Students on Some of Life's Ideals* (Henry Holt and Company, 1912), 65.

34 Wendy Wood, Jeffrey M. Quinn, and Deborah A. Kashy, "Habits in Everyday Life: Thought, Emotion, and Action," *Journal of Personality and Social Psychology* 83, no. 6 (2002): 1281–1297, https://doi.org/10.1037/0022-3514.83.6.1281.

35 Warren E. Buffett, "Chairman's Letter–1985," Berkshire Hathaway, March 4, 1986, https://www.berkshirehathaway.com/letters/1985.html.

36 Hal R. Arkes and Catherine Blumer, "The Psychology of Sunk Cost," *Organizational Behavior and Human Decision Processes* 35, no. 1 (February 1985): 126, https://doi.org/10.1016/0749-5978(85)90049-4.

37 Arkes and Blumer, "Psychology of Sunk Cost," 127.

38 Arthur Goldwag, "What UFO Cultists Can Teach Us About Political Paranoia Today," *Time*, March 26, 2024, https://time.com/6960441/ufo-cultists-political-paranoia-essay/.

39 Leon Festinger, Henry W. Riecken, and Stanley Schachter, *When Prophecy Fails* (University of Minnesota Press, 1956), 174–215.

40 Irvine Loudon, "Ignaz Philipp Semmelweis' Studies of Death in Childbirth," *Journal of the Royal Society of Medicine* 106, no. 11 (2013): 461–63.

41 Nicholas Kadar, Roberto Romero, and Zoltán Papp, "Ignaz Semmelweis: 'The Savior of Mothers': On the 200th Anniversary of the Birth," *American Journal of Obstetrics & Gynecology* 219, no. 6 (December 2018): 519–22, https://doi.org/10.1016/j.ajog.2018.10.036.

42 Francis Bacon, *Novum Organum: Book I* (Henry Regnery Company, 1949), 15.

43 Charles G. Lord, Lee Ross, and Mark R. Lepper, "Biased Assimilation and Attitude Polarization: The Effects of Prior Theories on Subsequently Considered Evidence," *Journal of Personality and Social Psychology* 37, no. 11 (1979): 2098–2109, https://doi.org/10.1037/0022-3514.37.11.2098.

44 Eugene Malthouse, "Confirmation Bias and Vaccine-Related Beliefs in the Time of COVID-19," *Journal of Public Health* 45, no. 2 (June 2023): 523–528, https://doi.org/10.1093/pubmed/fdac128.

45 Will Self, "Forget Fake News on Facebook—The Real Filter Bubble Is You," *The New Statesman*, November 28, 2016, https://www.newstatesman.com/science-tech/2016/11/forget-fake-news-facebook-real-filter-bubble-you.

46 Richard Dawkins, "Evidence-Based Life," *The Poetry of Reality with Richard Dawkins*, Substack, June 3, 2023, https://richarddawkins.substack.com/p/evidence-based-life.

47 Ralph Waldo Emerson, *Self-Reliance* (The Peter Pauper Press, 1967), 21.

48 Emerson, *Self-Reliance*, 21.

49 Charles K. Hofling et al., "An Experimental Study in Nurse-Physician Relationships," *Journal of Nervous and Mental Disease* 143, no. 2 (August 1966): 171–180, https://doi.org/10.1097/00005053-196608000-00008.

50 Hofling et al., "An Experimental Study in Nurse-Physician Relationships."

51 Solomon E. Asch, "Studies of Independence and Conformity: I. A Minority of One Against a Unanimous Majority," *Psychological Monographs: General and Applied* 70, no. 9 (1956): 58, https://doi.org/10.1037/h0093718.

52 Solomon E. Asch, "Studies of Independence and Conformity: I. A Minority of One against a Unanimous Majority," *Psychological Monographs: General and Applied* 70, no. 9 (1956).

53 Pew Research Center, "The Experiences of U.S. Adults Who Don't Have Children," July 25, 2024, https://www.pewresearch.org/social-trends/2024/07/25/the-experiences-of-u-s-adults-who-dont-have-children/.

54 Thomas Frank, *The Conquest of Cool: Business Culture, Counterculture, and the Rise of Hip Consumerism* (Chicago: University of Chicago Press, 1997), 7.

55 Stanley Milgram, "Behavioral Study of Obedience," *Journal of Abnormal and Social Psychology* 67, no. 4 (1963): 376, https://doi.org/10.1037/h0040525.

56 Craig Haney, Curtis Banks, and Philip Zimbardo, "Interpersonal Dynamics in a Simulated Prison," *International Journal of Criminology and Penology* 1, no. 1 (1973): 69–97, http://pdf.prisonexp.org/ijcp1973.pdf.

57 Hofling et al., "Nurse-Physician Relationships," 171–180.

58 Obergefell v. Hodges, 576 U.S. 644 (2015).

59 Richard H. Thaler and Cass R. Sunstein, *Nudge: Improving Decisions About Health, Wealth, and Happiness* (Penguin Books, 2009), 8.

60 Brigitte C. Madrian and Dennis F. Shea, "The Power of Suggestion: Inertia in 401(k) Participation and Savings Behavior," *Quarterly Journal of Economics* 116, no. 4 (2001): 1149–87.

61 Eric J. Johnson and Daniel Goldstein, "Do Defaults Save Lives?," *Science* 302, no. 5649 (2003): 1338, https://doi.org/10.1126/science.1091721.

62 Richard H. Thaler, "The Power of Nudges, for Good and Bad," *New York Times*, October 31, 2015, https://www.nytimes.com/2015/11/01/upshot/the-power-of-nudges-for-good-and-bad.html.

63 Bertrand Russell, *Marriage and Morals* (George Allen & Unwin, 1930), 50.

64 David Hume, *A Treatise of Human Nature*, ed. L. A. Selby-Bigge (Oxford University Press, 1960), 469–470.

65 Scott Eidelman, Christian S. Crandall, and Jennifer Pattershall, "The Existence Bias," *Journal of Personality and Social Psychology* 97, no. 5 (2009): 765–775, https://doi.org/10.1037/a0017058.

66 Scott Eidelman, Jennifer Pattershall, and Christian S. Crandall, "Longer Is Better," *Journal of Experimental Social Psychology* 46, no. 6 (November 2010): 993–998, https://doi.org/10.1016/j.jesp.2010.07.008.

67 Marion Andrivet, "New Coke: A Classic Branding Case Study on a Major Product Change Failure," *The Branding Journal*, February 10, 2025, https://www.thebrandingjournal.com/2025/02/new-coke/.

68 Adam H. Smiley and Matthew Fisher, "The Golden Age Is Behind Us: How the Status Quo Impacts the Evaluation of Technology," *Psychological Science* 33, no. 9 (2022): 1605–1614, https://doi.org/10.1177/09567976221102868.

69 Christian S. Crandall et al., "Status Quo Framing Increases Support for Torture," *Social Influence* 4, no. 1 (2009): 1–10, https://doi.org/10.1080/15534510802124397.

70 William Samuelson and Richard Zeckhauser, "Status Quo Bias in Decision Making," *Journal of Risk and Uncertainty* 1, no. 1 (1988): 7–59, https://doi.org/10.1007/BF00055564.

71 Adrian R. Camilleri and Sunita Sah, "Amplification of the Status Quo Bias Among Physicians Making Medical Decisions," *Applied Cognitive Psychology* 35, no. 6 (2021): 1374–1386, https://doi.org/10.1002/acp.3868.

72 Camilleri and Sah, "Amplification," 1379.

73 Annie Duke, *Quit: The Power of Knowing When to Walk Away* (Portfolio/Penguin, 2022), 151.

74 Melvin J. Lerner, *The Belief in a Just World: A Fundamental Delusion* (Plenum Press, 1980), 4–11.

75 John T. Jost and Mahzarin R. Banaji, "The Role of Stereotyping in System-Justification and the Production of False Consciousness," *British Journal of Social Psychology* 33, no. 1 (1994): 1–27, https://doi.org/10.1111/j.2044-8309.1994.tb01008.x.

76 Ashleigh S. Rosette, Geoffrey J. Leonardelli, and Katherine W. Phillips, "The White Standard: Racial Bias in Leader Categorization," *Journal of Applied Psychology* 93, no. 4 (2008): 758–77; Seval Gündemir et al., "Think Leader, Think White? Capturing and Weakening an Implicit Pro-White Leadership Bias," *PLoS ONE* 9, no. 1 (2014): e83915.

77 John T. Jost, Mahzarin R. Banaji, and Brian A. Nosek, "A Decade of System Justification Theory: Accumulated Evidence of Conscious and Unconscious Bolstering of the Status Quo," *Political Psychology* 25, no. 6 (2004): 881–919, https://doi.org/10.1111/j.1467-9221.2004.00402.x.

78 Milton Mayer, *They Thought They Were Free: The Germans 1933–45* (University of Chicago Press, 1967), 170–171.

79 Mayer, *They Thought*, 171–172.

80 Bertrand Russell, *The Conquest of Happiness* (George Allen & Unwin, 1932), 178.

81 Richard Pascale, Jerry Sternin, and Monique Sternin, *The Power of Positive Deviance: How Unlikely Innovators Solve the World's Toughest Problems* (Harvard Business Press, 2010), 33–37.

82 Pascale, Sternin, and Sternin, *Positive Deviance*, x.

83 Basma Albanna and Richard Heeks, "Positive Deviance, Big Data, and Development: A Systemic Literature Review," *The Electronic Journal of Information Systems in Developing Countries* 85, no. 1 (2018): 4, e12063, https://doi.org/10.1002/isd2.12063.

84 Arnold Schwarzenegger, "Athlete," episode 1 of *Arnold*, directed by Lesley Chilcott, aired June 7, 2023, on Netflix, 6:50–7:15.

85 Eddie Pells, "Dick Fosbury, High Jumper Who Created Now-Standard 'Fosbury Flop,' Dies at 76," *Los Angeles Times*, March 14, 2023, https://www.latimes.com/obituaries/story/2023-03-14/fosbury-flop-high-jumper-dick-fosbury-dead.

86 Richard Hoffer, *Something in the Air: American Passion and Defiance in the 1968 Mexico City Olympics* (Free Press, 2009), 74.

87 Arnold Schwarzenegger, "(Original) Arnold Schwarzenegger—The Speech That Broke the Internet—Most Inspiring Story Ever," moderated by Jürgen Höller, speech presented at Power Weekend 2018 for the Jürgen Höller Academy, posted December 8, 2018, by Jürgen Höller, YouTube, 00:30:29, https://www.youtube.com/watch?v=Px7bjMyPA30.

88 Adam Grant, *Originals: How Non-Conformists Move the World* (Penguin Books, 2016), 19.

89 Ted Williams and John Underwood, *The Science of Hitting* (Fireside, 1986), 37.

90 Roelof Botha, "Seed/Early + Growth," Sequoia, accessed October 7, 2025, https://www.sequoiacap.com/people/roelof-botha/.

91 Botha, "Seed/Early."

92 Matt Ridley, *Francis Crick: Discoverer of the Genetic Code* (Atlas Books, 2006), 208.

93 Warren E. Buffett, "Chairman's Letter—2022," Berkshire Hathaway, February 25, 2023, https://www.berkshirehathaway.com/letters/2022ltr.pdf.

94 Chaitanya Charan, "Comfortable Misery Is Still Misery," *Gita Daily* (blog), May 29, 2017, https://gitadaily.com/comfortable-misery-is-still-misery/.

95 Daniel T. Gilbert et al., "The Peculiar Longevity of Things Not So Bad," *Psychological Science* 15, no. 1 (2004): 14–19, https://doi.org/10.1111/j.0963-7214.2004.01501003.x.

96 Harry Bradford, "Fred Smith, FedEx Founder And CEO, Once Gambled $5,000 On Blackjack To Keep Company Alive," HuffPost, October 15, 2012, https://www.huffpost.com/entry/fred-smith-blackjack-fedex_n_1966837.

97 David Martin, "FedEx: A 50-Year Revolution of Business," CBS News, June 4, 2023, https://www.cbsnews.com/news/federal-express-fred-smith-50-years-of-fedex/.

98 Frederick W. Smith, quoted in *The Forbes Book of Business Quotations: 14,173 Thoughts on the Business of Life*, ed. Ted Goodman (New York: Black Dog & Leventhal, 1997), 451.

99 Henry D. Thoreau, *Walden; Or, Life in the Woods* (Ticknor and Fields, 1854), 10.

100 Paraphrased from Aristotle, *Metaphysics* 1.1 (7109–12), trans. Jonathan Barnes, in *The Complete Works of Aristotle*, ed. Jonathan Barnes (Princeton University Press, 1984).

101 David McCullough, *The Wright Brothers* (Simon & Schuster, 2015), 36–38, 53–58, 103.

102 David Kindy, "This Odd Early Flying Machine Made History But Didn't Have the Right Stuff," *Smithsonian Magazine*, May 5, 2021, https://www.smithsonianmag.com/smithsonian-institution/odd-early-flying-machine-made-history-didnt-have-right-stuff-180977658/.

103 Richard P. Feynman and Ralph Leighton, *"Surely You're Joking, Mr. Feynman!": Adventures of a Curious Character*, ed. Edward Hutchings (Vintage, 1992), 36–37.

104 Francis Crick, *What Mad Pursuit: A Personal View of Scientific Discovery* (Basic Books, 1988), 11.

105 F. H. C. Crick and L. E. Orgel, "Directed Panspermia," *Icarus* 19, no. 3 (July 1973): 341–346, https://doi.org/10.1016/0019-1035(73)90110-3.

106 Matt Ridley, *Francis Crick: Discoverer of the Genetic Code* (HarperCollins, 2006), 103.

107 Burkhard Bilger, "The Possibilian," *New Yorker*, April 18, 2011, https://www.newyorker.com/magazine/2011/04/25/the-possibilian?currentPage=all.

108 Adam Grant, "Christopher Nolan Wants You to Silence Your Phones," *Esquire*, July 19, 2017, https://www.esquire.com/entertainment/movies/a55985/christopher-nolan-interview/.

109 David Epstein, "Christopher Nolan Reads 'Without Purpose,'" *Range Widely*, Substack, August 3, 2023, https://davidepstein.substack.com/p/christopher-nolan-reads-without-purpose.

110 Matt Ridley, *Francis Crick: Discoverer of the Genetic Code* (Atlas Books, 2006), 17.

111 "Proposals and Queries to be Asked the Junto," preserved in *The Papers of Benjamin Franklin*, vol. 1 (New Haven: Yale University Press, 1959), doc. 89.

112 Benjamin Franklin, *The Autobiography of Benjamin Franklin* (Touchstone, 1997), 63–64.

113 Jack Canfield and Janet Switzer, *The Success Principles: How to Get from Where You Are to Where You Want to Be* (Collins, 2005), 189.

114 Mark Twain, *The Innocents Abroad* (American Publishing Company, 1899), 650.

115 Julia Cameron, *The Listening Path: The Creative Art of Attention* (St. Martin's Essentials, 2021), 20.

116 Cameron, *Listening Path*, 22.

117 John Steinbeck, *Travels with Charley: In Search of America* (Penguin Books, 2002), 208.

118   Tired (@_crustbag_), "I love that AC/DC was generally considered super rebellious at one point, and now their music is literally being used in Applebee's commercials," Twitter (now X), May 14, 2021, https://x.com/_crustbag_/status/1393382947084849152.

119   Steve Jobs, "'You've Got to Find What You Love,' Jobs Says," Stanford Report, June 12, 2005, https://news.stanford.edu/stories/2005/06/youve-got-find-love-jobs-says.

120   Jobs, "Find What You Love."

121   Jobs, "Find What You Love."

122   Jobs, "Find What You Love."

123   Jordi Quoidbach, Daniel T. Gilbert, and Timothy D. Wilson, "The End of History Illusion," *Science* 339, no. 6115 (2013): 96–98, https://doi.org/10.1126/science.1229294.

124   Ralph Waldo Emerson, "Experience," in *The Collected Works of Ralph Waldo Emerson*, vol. 3, *Essays: Second Series*, ed. Joseph Slater (Harvard University Press, 1979), 28.

125   David Epstein, "Pour Out Lesser Ideas to Get to Great Ones," *Range Widely*, Substack, June 22, 2023, https://davidepstein.substack.com/p/pour-out-lesser-ideas-to-get-to-greater.

126   Epstein, "Pour Out."

127   Epstein, "Pour Out."

128   Thomas Edison, "Famous Quotes by Thomas Edison," Thomas Edison Foundations, accessed October 7, 2025, https://www.thomasedison.org/edison-quotes.

129   Morgan Housel, "How to Read: Lots of Inputs and a Strong Filter," *Collab Fund* (blog), August 3, 2023, https://collabfund.com/blog/how-to-read-lots-of-inputs-and-a-strong-filter/?utm_source=chatgpt.com.

130   Housel, "How to Read."

131   Housel, "How to Read."

132   William Zinsser, *On Writing Well* (Quill, 2001), 238.

133   Johnny Depp and Marlow Stern, "Johnny Depp on Hunter S. Thompson," *Newsweek*, October 23, 2011, https://www.newsweek.com/johnny-depp-hunter-s-thompson-68201.

134   Bertrand Russell, *The Autobiography of Bertrand Russell: 1872–1914: Volume I* (George Allen and Unwin, 1971), 13.

135   Epictetus, *Enchiridion*, trans. George Long (Prometheus Books, 1997), 27.

136   Frank Lloyd Wright, "In the Cause of Architecture," *The Architectural Record* 23, no. 3 (March 1908): 157, https://www.architecturalrecord.com/ext/resources/news/2016/01-Jan/InTheCause/Frank-Lloyd-Wright-In-the-Cause-of-Architecture-March-1908.pdf.

137   Stefan Sagmeister, "The Power of Time Off," TEDGlobal, July 2009, video, https://www.ted.com/talks/stefan_sagmeister_the_power_of_time_off; Stefan Sagmeister, *Things I Have Learned in My Life So Far* (Abrams, 2008).

138   *Steve Jobs: One Last Thing*, directed by Sarah Hunt and Mimi O'Connor, narrated by Demetri Goritsas (PBS, 2011).

139   *Steve Jobs: One Last Thing*, directed by Sarah Hunt and Mimi O'Connor, narrated by Demetri Goritsas (PBS, 2011).

140 Neal Bascomb, *The Perfect Mile: Three Athletes, One Goal, and Less Than Four Minutes to Achieve It* (Houghton Mifflin, 2004), 72–74, 208–211.

141 Sieva Kozinsky, "I've Wasted a Lot of Time…Here's What I've Learned, and Some Lessons on Time & Energy That Will Help You in Your Business," *Sieva's Business Academy* (blog), February 21, 2024, https://www.sievakozinsky.com/new-archive/ive-wasted-a-lot-of-time-heres-what-ive-learned-and-some-lessons-on-time-energy-that-will-help-you-in-your-business.

142 Steven Pinker, "Groups of People May Differ Genetically in Their Average Talents and Temperaments," in *What Is Your Dangerous Idea?: Today's Leading Thinkers on the Unthinkable*, ed. John Brockman (Simon & Schuster, 2006), 13–16.

143 John Brockman, ed., *What Is Your Dangerous Idea? Today's Leading Thinkers on the Unthinkable* (New York: Harper Perennial, 2007), 13–16, 191–195, 223–224.

144 Daniel C. Dennett, *Breaking the Spell: Religion as a Natural Phenomenon* (Viking, 2006), 6.

145 Yvon Chouinard, "Earth Is Now Our Only Shareholder," Patagonia, September 14, 2022, https://www.patagonia.com/ownership/?utm_source=chatgpt.com.

146 George T. Doran, "There's a S.M.A.R.T. Way to Write Management's Goals and Objectives," *Management Review* 70, no. 11 (1981): 35–36.

147 Kathleen D. Vohs et al., "Making Choices Impairs Subsequent Self-Control: A Limited-Resource Account of Decision Making, Self-Regulation, and Active Initiative," *Journal of Personality and Social Psychology* 94, no. 5 (2008): 883–898, https://doi.org/10.1037/0022-3514.94.5.883.

148 William Samuelson and Richard Zeckhauser, "Status Quo Bias in Decision Making," *Journal of Risk and Uncertainty* 1, no. 1 (1988): 7–59, https://doi.org/10.1007/BF00055564.

149 Barry Schwartz, *The Paradox of Choice: Why More Is Less* (New York: Harper Perennial, 2004), esp. chs. 5–6.

150 Vilfredo Pareto, *Cours d'économie politique*, vol. 2 (Lausanne: F. Rouge, 1897), 299; see also Joseph M. Juran, *Managerial Breakthrough* (New York: McGraw-Hill, 1964), 26–28, for the later "Pareto principle" formulation.

151 William Zinsser, *On Writing Well* (Quill, 2001), 18.

152 Gary Keller and Jay Papasan, *The One Thing: The Surprisingly Simple Truth Behind Extraordinary Results* (Bard Press, 2014), 55.

153 K. M. Sheldon and A. J. Elliot, "Goal Striving, Need Satisfaction, and Longitudinal Well-Being: The Self-Concordance Model," *Journal of Personality and Social Psychology* 76, no. 3 (1999): 482–497, https://doi.org/10.1037/0022-3514.76.3.482.

154 Andre Agassi, *Open: An Autobiography* (Alfred A. Knopf, 2009), 3.

155 Bill Copeland, quoted in *The Yale Book of Quotations*, ed. Fred R. Shapiro (Yale University Press, 2006), 166.

156 Baidhurya Mani, "The 30 Must-Know Subscription Economy Statistics in 2024," Sell Courses Online, last updated February 20, 2024, https://sellcoursesonline.com/subscription-economy-statistics?utm_source=chatgpt.com.

157 E. B. White, *Essays of E. B. White* (Harper Colophon Books, 1979), 4.

158 Robert Waldinger and Marc Schulz, *The Good Life: Lessons from the World's Longest Scientific Study of Happiness* (Simon and Schuster, 2023), 10.

159 Benjamin Hardy, *Willpower Doesn't Work: Discover the Hidden Keys to Success* (Hachette Books, 2019), 86.

160 David Goggins, *Can't Hurt Me: Master Your Mind and Defy the Odds* (Lioncrest Publishing, 2018), 11.

161 Goggins, *Can't Hurt Me*.

162 Carol S. Dweck, *Mindset: How Can You Fulfil Your Potential* (Robinson, 2012), 6–7.

163 Henry D. Thoreau, *Walden; Or, Life in the Woods* (Ticknor and Fields, 1854), 98.

164 Derek Sivers, *Anything You Want: 40 Lessons for a New Kind of Entrepreneur* (Do You Zoom, 2011), 11.

165 Seneca, *Letters from a Stoic*, trans. Robin Campbell (London: Penguin Classics, 1969), Letter 13.

166 "Lawrence Ferlinghetti Discusses the Publication of 'Howl:' ACLU Banned Books Week 2001," ACLU, February 27, 2002, https://www.aclu.org/documents/lawrence-ferlinghetti-discusses-publication-howl-aclu-banned-books-week-2001.

167 Rick Rubin, *The Creative Act: A Way of Being* (New York: Penguin Press, 2023), 5.

168 Jim Carrey, "Commencement Speech Transcript 2014 at Maharishi University of Management," Rev, May 30, 2014, https://www.rev.com/transcripts/jim-carrey-commencement-speech-transcript-2014-at-maharishi-university-of-management.

169 Matt Zeigler, "David Letterman's Advice To Jerry Seinfeld," Cultish Creative, May 16, 2024, https://cultishcreative.com/p/david-lettermans-advice-jerry-seinfeld.

170 Kathrine Switzer, *Marathon Woman: Running the Race to Revolutionize Women's Sports* (Carroll & Graf Publishers, 2007), 91.

171 Switzer, *Marathon Woman*, 93.

172 "Lady with Desire to Run Crashed Marathon," Sports, *New York Times*, April 23, 1967, p. 199, https://www.nytimes.com/1967/04/23/archives/lady-with-desire-to-run-crashed-marathon-officials-at-boston-shaken.html.

173 Myron Cope, "Angry Overseer of the Marathon," *Sports Illustrated*, April 22, 1968, https://vault.si.com/vault/1968/04/22/angry-overseer-of-the-marathon.

174 Kathrine Switzer, *Marathon Woman: Running the Race to Revolutionize Women's Sports* (Cambridge, MA: Da Capo Press, 2007), 274.

175 Switzer, *Marathon Woman*, 48.

176 Switzer, *Marathon Woman*, 9.

177 Switzer, *Marathon Woman*, 50.

www.ingramcontent.com/pod-product-compliance
Lightning Source LLC
LaVergne TN
LVHW041958060526
838200LV00019B/381/J